THE WEIGHT OF GLORY
AND OTHER ADDRESSES

By C. S. Lewis

The Abolition of Man
Mere Christianity
The Great Divorce
The Problem of Pain
The Weight of Glory and Other Addresses
The Screwtape Letters (with "Screwtape Proposes a Toast")
Miracles
The Case for Christianity
The Lion, the Witch and the Wardrobe
Prince Caspian
The Voyage of the Dawn Treader
The Silver Chair
The Magician's Nephew
The Horse and His Boy
The Last Battle
Perelandra
That Hideous Strength
Out of the Silent Planet
The Joyful Christian
George Macdonald: An Anthology

About C. S. Lewis:

Through Joy and Beyond: A Pictorial Biography of C. S. Lewis,
    by Walter Hooper
Past Watchful Dragons: The Narnian Chronicles of C. S. Lewis,
    by Walter Hooper
*They Stand Together: The Letters of C. S. Lewis to Arthur Greeves
    (1914-1963),* edited by Walter Hooper
C. S. Lewis at the Breakfast Table and Other Reminiscences,
    edited by James T. Como

Available at your local bookstore or from Macmillan Publishing
Company, 100K Brown Street, Riverside, NJ 08370

THE WEIGHT OF GLORY

AND OTHER ADDRESSES

C. S. LEWIS

REVISED AND EXPANDED EDITION

Edited, and with an Introduction, by

WALTER HOOPER

Collier Books
MACMILLAN PUBLISHING COMPANY
New York

*Macmillan Publishing Company
866 Third Avenue, New York, N.Y. 10022*

*Library of Congress Cataloging in Publication Data
Lewis, Clive Staples, 1898-1963.
The weight of glory and other addresses.
Contents: The weight of glory. Learning.
War-time—Why I am not a pacifist. [etc.]
I. Theology—Addresses—A. essays, lectures
I. Hooper, Walter   II. Title
BR50.L396 1980   230   80-18792
ISBN 0—02—095980—X (pbk.)*

*First Paperback Edition of
Revised and Expanded Edition 1980*

10   9   8   7   6   5   4

*Macmillan Books are available at special discounts
for bulk purshases for sales promotions, premiums,
fund-raising, or educational use.
For details, contact:*

*Special Sales Director
Macmillan Publishing Company
866 Third Avenue
New York, N.Y. 10022*

Printed in the United States of America

CONTENTS

INTRODUCTION

In his beautiful peroration at the end of his sermon "The Weight of Glory," C. S. Lewis, after commenting on the immortality of the human soul, says, "This does not mean that we are to be perpetually solemn. We must play. But our merriment must be of that kind (and it is, in fact, the merriest kind) which exists between people who have, from the outset, taken each other seriously."

I believe that this and similar encouragements by Lewis contribute significantly to the subject of what constitutes Christian behaviour. Having done the best we can to perform whatever God demands, should we not at least enjoy the good He sends us? Willing ourselves to be "perpetually solemn" when there is no reason for it seems to me not only a rejection of the happiness we could have on earth, but also to jeopardise our capacity to enjoy it in the future when every possible reason for unhappiness has been finally swept away.

We know from his earliest writings that Lewis was born with a sense of fun, and that it was considerably maimed by an entanglement of atheism and ambition. Perhaps a fiercely serious ambition for whatever it might be can never live in harmony with the merriment he describes. Certainly, Lewis could write no great works until he was converted to Christianity in 1931, after which he ceased to take much interest in himself. If it is objected by those of a lugubrious disposition that the Christian religion *is* serious and of great solemnity, then my answer is, "Yes, of course. And not taken seriously enough." But Lewis comes to our rescue at this point by showing us in his book *The Four Loves* how easily things can become other than they should be through the wrong *kind* of seriousness.

In editing these essays I have been led to reflect on that ever mysterious, but instinctive notion we seem to be born with that tells us just how merry, how serious, how whatever you will, we know we can be with someone else. My relation to Lewis may be similar to that of others, but it can't be exactly like. As this book is being edited primarily for Americans, I should explain that after I had corresponded with Lewis for some years, he invited me to come over in the spring of 1963 from my native United States for what I hoped would be as much as a single conversation over a cup of tea. I don't believe in luck, but I do believe in angels, and the coveted tea party turned out to be (if it needs a name) "The Observations of a Late Arrival" or "A Single Summer with C.S.L." In any event, as the sources of our first-hand evidence about him decrease with the years, I hope that mine will be of some interest to those who feel as I do about that merriment "of the merriest kind" of which there seems no abundance these days.

It took some time for an American, such as myself, to adapt to English "conveniences." I see, for instance, from my diary of 7 June 1963 that during a longish visit with Lewis we drank what seemed gallons of tea. After a while I asked to be shown the "bathroom," forgetting that in most homes the bathroom and the toilet are separate rooms. With a kind of mock formality, Lewis showed me to the bathroom, pointed to the tub, flung down a pile of towels, and closed the door behind me. I returned to his sitting-room to say that it was not a *bath* I wanted but. . . . "Well, sir, 'choose you this day,' " said Lewis, bursting with laughter as he quoted the prophet Joshua, "*that* will break you of those silly American euphemisms. And now, *where* is it you wanted to go?"

I see from other entries I made that Lewis—or "Jack" as he preferred to be called by his friends— and I were meeting at least three or four times a week, sometimes at his house, at other times in a pub with a group of friends called "The Inklings." I knew that he was ill, indeed, that he had been so since 1961 when the troubles with his health began. He, however, seemed to think little of it and, as he looked so robust, it was easy to forget it when in company with this ruddy, six-foot, genial man. Hence the surprise of finding him not well enough to attend Mass with me on July 14. He urged me to remain there with him, and this was a memorable day for me in more ways than one. It was then that he asked me to accept immediately a post as his literary assistant and personal secretary, and later, after resigning my teaching position at the University of Kentucky, to return to Oxford to resume my duties.

Lewis went for a routine examination the next morning to the Acland Nursing Home, and, much to everyone's surprise, he sank into a coma, lasting about twenty-four hours, from which the doctors did not believe he would recover. Our mutual friends, the Reverend Dr. Austin Farrer and his wife, were to be on holiday in Wales from the sixteenth through the thirty-first of July, but at Lewis's request they remained in Oxford until the seventeenth, so that Austin Farrer could hear his confession and give him the Blessed Sacrament. Lewis wanted me to receive the Sacrament with him, but as I was not ill, this was not allowed. "In that case," Lewis said, "you must be present to do the kneeling for me." With so much to do for him at this time I was unable to keep a regular diary. However, I see from a letter I wrote to the Farrers on July 30 from Lewis's home, and now part of the Farrer Papers in the Bodleian Library, Oxford, that I had already moved into Lewis's home by that time.

Rather than tell Lewis how close he had come to dying, the doctors appeared to leave this to me. When I judged the time to be right, I told him about the coma and the few days when his mind was disordered. Thereafter Lewis continued to believe that the Extreme Unction administered during the coma and his reception of the Blessed Sacrament had saved his life.

Even before he went into the nursing home I marvelled that Lewis had lived so long without setting himself ablaze. Except when he dressed for a special occasion, he wore an old tweed jacket, the right-hand pocket of which had been patched and re-patched many times. This was because Lewis, when wearied of his pipe, would drop it into his pocket, with the result that it would burn its way through. And this happened so often that there was none of the original material left.

The nurses in the Acland, having found him nodding with a cigarette in his hand, would have none of this. And so it was that, except when I was with him, they would not allow him to have any matches. What puzzled Lewis was that after I had left him with a box of matches, a nurse would, as soon as I left, rush in and take them away. "How do they *know*?" he asked me one morning. "Give me a box I can hide under my bedclothes." I had then to confess that while I was the supplier, I was also the informer. "Informer!" roared Lewis. "I have what no friend ever had before. I have a private traitor, my very own personal Benedict Arnold. Repent before it is too late!"

I loved all the rough and tumble of this, and I fancy I pulled his leg about as often as he pulled mine. But there was the gentler side that was just as typical. There was one incident that took place in the Acland which the readers of his Narnian stories might find as endearing as I did. It occurred on one of those days when Lewis's mind was disordered and when, as I noticed, he could not recognise any of those who dropped in to see him—not even Professor Tolkien. The last visitor of the day was his foster-sister, Maureen Moore Blake, who a few months previously, and by a very unexpected turn of events, had become Lady Dunbar of Hempriggs, with a castle and a vast estate in Scotland. She was the first woman in three centuries to succeed to a baronetcy. They had not met since this happened and, hoping to spare her any disappointment, I told her that he had not been able to recognise any of his old friends. He opened his eyes when she took his hand. "Jack," she whispered, "it is Maureen." "No," replied Lewis smiling, "it is Lady Dunbar of Hempriggs." "Oh, Jack, how could you remember that?" she asked. "On the contrary," he said. "How could *I* forget a fairy tale?"

One day when he was obviously much better, but

not completely out of danger, he asked why I looked so glum.

The reason for the glumness was that, living in our neighbourhood was a fierce old atheist of about ninety-seven who went out for a brisk walk every day. Whenever we met he asked if Lewis was "still alive," and on receiving my reply that he was indeed quite ill, he invariably said, "Nothing wrong with *me*! I've got a long time yet!"

I told Lewis that I was tempted—very strongly tempted—to tell Our Lord that I thought it monstrously unfair that He should allow the naughty old atheist to seemingly go on forever and yet let Lewis, who was only sixty-four, come so close to the point of death. "Mind you," I said, observing Lewis's face cloud over, "I haven't actually *said* it in my prayers, but I've come pretty close."

"And what do you think Our Lord would say to that?" Lewis said with a discouraging look.

"What?"

"What is that to *you*!"

Anyone who has read St. John 21:22—Our Lord's rebuke to St. Peter—will recognise Lewis's application of it in this instance. And then tenderly, tenderly, Lewis comforted me in what I had imagined was his sorrow, but which he knew was mine.

The worst over, there was a return of the high spirits and uproarious sense of fun that I found one of the most attractive things about Lewis. But it would take someone of Boswell's talents to give the right idea to the completeness of this remarkable man, to show how naturally the humour blended into the more serious side, and indeed was one of the *causes* of his greatness of heart, his large intellect, and the most open charity I have ever found in anyone. He was a man, many of us have come to see, of common instincts combined with very uncommon abilities. Perhaps it is worth recording that I knew—I just *knew*—that no matter how long I lived, no matter who else I met, I should never be in the company of such a supremely good human being again. Of all my memories this is the most indelible and is certain to remain so.

I brought Lewis home on August 6, along with a male nurse, a Scotsman named Alec Ross, whose responsibility it was to stay awake nights should he be needed. Lewis and I had been together almost continuously for two months, and I was even more comfortable with him now that we were in the same house. He had not once complained about conditions in the Acland—excepting, of course, my "traitorous" behaviour over the appearing and disappearing matches. Certainly he snuggled back into his familiar surroundings with much pleasure. Sensing that he liked being left alone a little while after lunch, I asked if he ever took a nap. "Oh, no!" he replied. "But, mind you, sometime a nap takes *me*."

He had kept up his dictating of letters during his stay in the Acland. And although he was able to do more of this at home, he gave as well more attention to the problems which, since 1961, he knew could become worse should he die suddenly: his brother's unfortunate problem with alcohol, and the future of his two stepsons who had, besides losing their mother in 1960, seen other sadnesses as well. But I mention these things because it was then I observed something I had never seen in anyone else (excepting, as I was to learn later, his friend Owen Barfield). Lewis had his share—some would say more than his share—of worries. But, having done all in his power to solve them, he left the matter to God and got on with his work and pleasures. Those who go on to read, for example, the additions to his sermon "Transposition" (of which more later) will perhaps understand what may sound like sweet banality but isn't—that Lewis really wanted and *liked* the happiness which the Divine Son died to give all men. And this I observed at the time, some ten years before I saw in the Bodleian the whole thing put so succinctly in a letter to his brother of 28 January 1940 in which he says, "I begin to suspect that the world is divided not only into the happy and the unhappy, but into those who *like* happiness and those who, odd as it seems, really don't." Without meaning any offence, I suspect that those who carry on about "social consciousness" or whatever the current jargon is would not understand this. Still, that is the way it was.

Our nurse hardly knew what to make of Lewis. Alec was not a learned man, but he was fortunate in being one of the few male nurses at that time. And for this reason he had been able to pick and choose his patients, nearly always with an eye as to whether they were fabulously rich, famous for something or the other, and (he hoped) possessed of a Rolls Royce. He was a good nurse but he had a foul tongue. At his first sight of the kitchen he pronounced the house to be a "pig sty" and very quickly had the servants sweeping, mopping, and disinfecting as fast as it could be done.

But there remained for him the mystifying contradiction of a far from attractive house presided over by a "somebody." We were taking our tea alone one day when he asked whether—he couldn't think of the name *Who's Who*—the "great mon was in that big boke . . ." Lewis was coming through the door and, overhearing this, said, "Ay, ay, Alec. I am in what you in Scotland would call *Wha's Wha*." That did it. Alec was thereafter devoted to Lewis for his humour and self-forgetfulness, it now making no difference whether Lewis was famous for anything Alec thought important.

In August Lewis dictated a letter announcing his retirement from Cambridge. Then, at the end of the month, with Alec left to keep an eye on Lewis, his stepson Douglas Gresham and I were sent to Cambridge to sort out his affairs and bring home many of the two thousand or so books from his Magdalene College rooms. This done, we hired a lorry to transport us and the books to Oxford. All the way home I wondered where the books could go in a house already filled to the bursting point. But Lewis had laid his plans.

Alec occupied what was called the "music room" —a large room on the ground floor, empty except for a bed in one corner. Having been up all night, Alec was asleep when we arrived. As the lorry pulled into the drive, there was Lewis cautioning us to be quiet. "Where'll we store the books?" I whispered. Lewis answered with a wink. With infinite pains so as not to waken Alec, we spent an hour or so carrying the books into the "music room" and stacking them around the nurse's bed. He was still snoring when the last one was added to the great wall of books, which was nearly as high as the ceiling and which filled nearly every square inch of the room.

About the time the nurse usually woke, Lewis and I were waiting outside for the results. Then it happened. Alec woke, found himself entombed in books, and bellowed at the top of his voice. Suddenly part of the great wall of books tumbled down, and a body scrambled out. Over drinks Alec pronounced it to be the best d———d joke he had seen played on anyone.

If I have said less than some would wish about Lewis's specifically "religious" position, that is because I assume that it is already quite clear. Rather, I have tried to indicate from personal recollections that Dr. Johnson might well have had such a man as C. S. Lewis in mind in suggesting that "the size of a man's understanding might always be justly measured by his mirth." If I have failed, then the splendid pieces that comprise this collection ought, as they say, "to make up for everything."

Lewis was a truly modest man. If his books came naturally into our conversation, he would talk about them with the same detachment as in discussing some stranger's works. But he had no interest as far as I could see in his literary or theological position in the world. One evening this came up rather naturally.

We had been talking about one of our favourite books, Malory's *Morte d'Arthur*, and I mentioned how disappointed I sometimes felt when, say, Sir Launcelot went out to deliver a helpless lady from some peril or other. Then, just at that point where you can't admire him enough for his selflessness, he explains to someone, as though it was the most natural thing in the world, that he is doing it to "win worship"—that is, to increase his reputation. We recognised it as an inheritance from Paganism. Without intending any embarrassment, I asked Lewis if he was ever aware of the fact that regardless of his intentions he was "winning worship" from his books. He said in a low, still voice, and with the deepest and most complete humility I've ever observed in anyone, "One cannot be too careful *not* to think of it." The house, the garden, the whole universe seemed hushed for a moment, and then we began talking again.

As those poignantly happy months drew to an end, and the time came for me to return to the United States, Lewis and I began planning for his retirement: the books he would write, the duties I would relieve him of, our study together of the old French sources that lie behind Malory's *Morte*. Even now, years later, those happy prospects have the power to tease me with such hopes as Lewis's Jill thought of in *The Last Battle* when "the picture of all those happy years . . . piled up . . . till it was rather like looking down from a high hill on to a rich, lovely plain full of woods and waters and cornfields, which spread away and away till it got thin and misty from distance." But Lewis died suddenly on 22 November 1963.

At times, when asked about him, I have made it clear that I was with him for "only" three months. But I think I do a disservice to both his memory and his kindness by that word *only*. Have we not all felt a lasting bond with someone we have known only minutes, and yet failed—for such is the nature of things—to achieve any intimacy with those we have run into for half an hour or so over a period of years? Make of it what you will. I am ashamed to admit that I once thought that because the plans Lewis and I made together did not run on into the years, I was somehow cheated. If not wicked, it is ungracious. Recently, the grandmother of one of my friends was dying, and I went with him into those delectable peaks of Derbyshire where the people are as free from cant and overstatement as any I know. It was early spring and there was nothing my friend could find for his grandmother but a few sprigs of pussy willow. As he gave them to her, minutes before she died, she pressed them to her face and whispered, "They're grand, my love. And enough."

But of his books there never seemed enough for Lewis's publishers. Yet much as Lewis loved to write, never was it, as it is with so many others, "zeal not according to knowledge." He had to have something to say before he put pen to paper. Still, although he kept to deadlines set by himself regarding his books, it took the initiative of his English and American publishers to press him into preparing selections of his shorter pieces. Not because Lewis had not put all his effort into such addresses as are found here, but he needed prodding before such selections were made.

This volume, consisting originally of the addresses numbered 1, 2, 4, 6, and 7, was published by Geoffrey Bles of London in 1949 under the title *Transposition and Other Addresses* and later that same year by Macmillan of New York as *The Weight of Glory and Other Addresses*. Since that time the volumes of essays on the two sides of the Atlantic have differed somewhat, and this book is an attempt to put things right. What spurred me into action was a tour I made of the United States in 1979 with the film *Through Joy and Beyond: The Life of C. S. Lewis*. After the film I ended the evening by reading aloud a portion of Lewis's "Transposition." What I had forgotten, and many

nice people reminded me of, was that what I considered one of the most ravishing pieces of prose
Lewis ever wrote had been added later, and was not
therefore in the American version. Although this
in itself was enough to justify resetting the text of
the book, it occurred to me that it also afforded the
ideal occasion for enlarging the volume by three
addresses never published in the United States and
one never published anywhere before.

The addresses are arranged chronologically except for (1) "The Weight of Glory" which is so
magnificent that not only do I dare to consider it
worthy of a place with some of the Church Fathers,
but I fear I should be hanged by Lewis's admirers
if it were not given primacy of place. It was
preached at the invitation of Canon T. R. Milford
at Solemn Evensong in the twelfth-century Oxford
University Church of St. Mary the Virgin on 8
June 1941 to one of the largest congregations ever
assembled there in modern times. Canon Milford,
who was the Vicar of St. Mary's, told me that the
invitation sprang from his reading of Lewis's *The
Pilgrim's Regress*. The sermon was published first
in *Theology*, vol. 43 (November 1941), and afterwards as a pamphlet by the S.P.C.K. in 1942.

(2) "Learning in War-Time" was also preached
at the invitation of Canon Milford at Evensong in
St. Mary the Virgin on 22 October 1939. This, too,
was owing to the Canon's appreciation of *The
Pilgrim's Regress* and, as he told me, because with
so much unrest caused to Oxford undergraduates by
World War II, Lewis—an ex-soldier and Christian
don at Magdalen College—was thought to be just
the man to put things into the right perspective. It
too brought a great crowd to St. Mary's, and Canon

Milford arranged for everyone present to be given a mimeographed copy of the sermon bearing the title *"None Other Gods": Culture in War-Time*. Lewis took as his text for the sermon Deut. 26:5— "A Syrian ready to perish was my father." It was published that same year, in pamphlet form under the title *The Christian in Danger*, by the Student Christian Movement.

(3) It was while this book was in preparation that my friend, George Sayer, a pupil of Lewis's at Magdalen during the war years and an intimate friend thereafter, sent me a copy of "Why I Am Not a Pacifist." The talk was given to a pacifist society in Oxford sometime in 1940, and Lewis made a copy for Mr. Sayer, a most fortuitous event as the original has not survived. We know that Lewis never made any attempt to publish it, and it appears in print here for the first time.

(4) "Transposition" was preached in the chapel of Mansfield College, Oxford—a Congregational institution—at the invitation of its Principal, Nathaniel Micklem (1888–1976), on the Feast of Pentecost, 28 May 1944. It was reported in *The Daily Telegraph* of 2 June 1944 under the heading "Modern Oxford's Newman" that "in the middle of the sermon Mr. Lewis, under stress of emotion, stopped, saying, 'I'm sorry,' and left the pulpit. Dr. Micklem, the Principal, and the chaplain went to his assistance. After a hymn was sung, Mr. Lewis returned and finished his sermon . . . on a deeply moving note."

Lewis has probably accomplished as much as any modern writer, both in his fiction and in his sermons, to make Heaven believable. My guess is that at sometime, but not necessarily in 1944, he may have felt that he had not succeeded as well as he might with "Transposition." Though he was quite ill during the spring of 1961 when Jock Gibb, his publisher at Geoffrey Bles, was pressing him to edit a volume of his essays, something wonderful happened. With a simplicity that is perhaps an instance of Heaven coming to its own rescue, Lewis was shown what glories are involved by the corruptible putting on incorruption, and there came from his pen an additional portion that raises that sermon to an eminence all its own. This new portion begins on p. 66 with the paragraph "I believe that this doctrine of Transposition provides . . ." and concludes on p. 69 with the paragraph ending, "They are too flimsy, too transitory, too phantasmal." This extended version of the sermon first appeared in Lewis's *They Asked for a Paper* (London, 1962).

(5) "Is Theology Poetry?" was read to the Oxford University Socratic Club on 6 November 1944 and was first published in *The Socratic Digest*, vol. 3 (1945). (6) "The Inner Ring" was the annual "Commemoration Oration" given at King's College, University of London, on 14 December 1944. (7) "Membership" was read to the Society of St. Alban and St. Sergius, Oxford, on 10 February 1945 at the invitation of Miss Anne Spalding, an old friend of Charles Williams, as it was in Miss Spalding's parents' home that Williams lived when he moved to Oxford at the outbreak of World War II. The paper was originally published in *Sobornost*, no. 31 (June 1945).

(8) "On Forgiveness" was written at the request of Father Patrick Kevin Irwin (1907–1965) and sent to him on 28 August 1947 for inclusion in

Father Irwin's parish magazine of the Church of St. Mary, Sawston, Cambridgeshire. However, Father Irwin was transferred to the Church of St. Augustine, Wisbech, before it could be published, and I first heard of the essay in 1975 when members of the priest's family deposited the manuscript in the Bodleian Library. It was first published in Lewis's *Fern-seed and Elephants and Other Essays on Christianity* (London: Fount/Collins, 1975).

(9) "A Slip of the Tongue" was the last sermon Lewis preached. It was given at the invitation of the Chaplain of Magdalene College, Cambridge, Father C. A. Pierce, in the college chapel at Evensong on 29 January 1956. Unlike Magdalen College, Oxford, the Cambridge college is quite small, and its chapel, a perfect little gem by candlelight, is indeed tiny. Even so, the Chapel Register reveals that it was crowded with so many people— one hundred—that extra seats had to be brought in. The sermon was published in *Screwtape Proposes a Toast and Other Pieces* (London: Fount/Collins, 1965), which volume Lewis was helping his publisher plan just before he died.

I am grateful to Collins Publishers for permission to reprint "Is Theology Poetry?" "On Forgiveness," and "A Slip of the Tongue," and to Mr. Sayer for providing me with a copy of "Why I Am Not a Pacifist." My thanks also to Owen Barfield for permitting me to edit this book and for all the other things that cause me to regard him as one of those friends who, by any reckoning, is one of the most obvious boasts of our fallen race.

27 March 1980　　　　WALTER HOOPER
Oxford

PREFACE

This book contains a selection of the too numerous addresses which I was induced to give during the late war and the years that immediately followed it. All were composed in response to personal requests and for particular audiences, without thought of subsequent publication. As a result, in one or two places they seem to repeat, though they really anticipated, sentences of mine which have already appeared in print. When I was asked to make this collection I supposed that I could remove such overlappings, but I was mistaken. There comes a time (and it need not always be a long one) when a composition belongs so definitely to the past that the author himself cannot alter it much without the feeling that he is producing a kind of forgery. The period from which these pieces date was, for all of us, an exceptional one; and though I do not think I have altered any belief that they embody I could not now recapture the tone and temper in which they were written. Nor would those who wanted to have them in a permanent form be pleased with a patchwork. It has therefore seemed better to let them go with only a few verbal corrections.

I have to thank the S.P.C.K., the S.C.M., and the proprietors of *Sobornost* for their kind permission to reprint *Weight of Glory*, *Learning in War-Time*, and *Membership*, respectively. *The Inner Ring* here appears in print for the first time. A different version of *Transposition*, written expressly for that purpose and then translated into Italian, has appeared in the *Rivista* of Milan.

C.S.L.

THE WEIGHT OF GLORY
AND OTHER ADDRESSES

THE WEIGHT
OF GLORY

If you asked twenty good men today what they thought the highest of the virtues, nineteen of them would reply, Unselfishness. But if you had asked almost any of the great Christians of old, he would have replied, Love. You see what has happened? A negative term has been substituted for a positive, and this is of more than philological importance. The negative idea of Unselfishness carries with it the suggestion not primarily of securing good things for others, but of going without them ourselves, as if our abstinence and not their happiness was the important point. I do not think this is the Christian virtue of Love. The New Testament has lots to say about self-denial, but not about self-denial as an end in itself. We are told to deny ourselves and to take up our crosses in order that we may follow Christ; and to nearly every description of what we shall ultimately find if we do so contains an appeal to desire. If there lurks in most modern minds the notion that to desire our own good and earnestly to hope for the enjoyment of it is a bad thing, I submit that this notion has crept in from Kant and the Stoics and is no part of the Christian faith. Indeed, if we consider the unblushing promises of reward and the staggering nature of the rewards promised in the Gospels, it would seem that Our Lord finds our desires not too strong, but too weak. We are half-hearted creatures, fooling about with drink and sex and ambition when infinite joy is offered us, like an ignorant child who wants to go on making mud pies in a slum because he cannot imagine what is meant by the offer of a holiday at the sea. We are far too easily pleased.

We must not be troubled by unbelievers when they say that this promise of reward makes the Christian life a mercenary affair. There are different kinds of rewards. There is the reward which has no natural connection with the things you do to earn it and is quite foreign to the desires that ought to accompany those things. Money is not the natural reward of love; that is why we call a man mercenary if he marries a woman for the sake of her money. But marriage is the proper reward for a real lover, and he is not mercenary for desiring it. A general who fights well in order to get a peerage is mercenary; a general who fights for victory is not, victory being the proper reward of battle as marriage is the proper reward of love. The proper rewards are not simply tacked on to the activity for which they are given, but are the activity itself in consummation. There is also a third case, which is more complicated. An enjoyment of Greek poetry is certainly a proper, and not a mercenary, reward for learning Greek; but only those who have reached the stage of enjoying Greek poetry can tell from their own experience that this is so. The schoolboy beginning Greek grammar cannot look forward to his adult enjoyment of Sophocles as a lover looks forward to marriage or a general to victory. He has to begin by working for marks, or to escape punishment, or to please his parents, or, at best, in the hope of a future good which he cannot at present imagine or desire. His position, therefore, bears a certain resemblance to that of the mercenary; the reward he is going to get will, in actual fact, be a natural or proper reward, but he will not know that till he has got it. Of course, he gets it gradually; enjoyment creeps in upon the mere drudgery, and nobody could point to a day or an hour when the one ceased and the other began. But it is just insofar as he approaches the reward that he becomes able to desire it for its own sake; indeed, the power of so desiring it is itself a preliminary reward.

The Christian, in relation to heaven, is in much the same position as this schoolboy. Those who have attained everlasting life in the vision of God doubtless know very well that it is no mere bribe, but the very consummation of their earthly discipleship; but we who have not yet attained it cannot know this in the same way, and cannot even begin to know it at all except by continuing to obey and finding the first reward of our obedience in our increasing power to desire the ultimate reward. Just in proportion as the desire grows, our fear lest it should be a mercenary desire will die away and finally be recognised as an absurdity. But probably this will not, for most of us, happen in a day; poetry replaces grammar, gospel replaces law, longing transforms obedience, as gradually as the tide lifts a grounded ship.

But there is one other important similarity between the schoolboy and ourselves. If he is an imaginative boy, he will, quite probably, be revelling in the English poets and romancers suitable to his age some time before he begins to suspect that Greek grammar is going to lead him to more and more enjoyments of this same sort. He may

even be neglecting his Greek to read Shelley and
Swinburne in secret. In other words, the desire
which Greek is really going to gratify already exists
in him and is attached to objects which seem to
him quite unconnected with Xenophon and the
verbs in μι. Now, if we are made for heaven, the
desire for our proper place will be already in us,
but not yet attached to the true object, and will
even appear as the rival of that object. And this, I
think, is just what we find. No doubt there is one
point in which my analogy of the schoolboy breaks
down. The English poetry which he reads when he
ought to be doing Greek exercises may be just as
good as the Greek poetry to which the exercises
are leading him, so that in fixing on Milton instead
of journeying on to Aeschylus his desire is not em-
bracing a false object. But our case is very different.
If a transtemporal, transfinite good is our real des-
tiny, then any other good on which our desire fixes
must be in some degree fallacious, must bear at
best only a symbolical relation to what will truly
satisfy.

In speaking of this desire for our own far-off
country, which we find in ourselves even now, I feel
a certain shyness. I am almost committing an inde-
cency. I am trying to rip open the inconsolable
secret in each one of you—the secret which hurts
so much that you take your revenge on it by calling
it names like Nostalgia and Romanticism and Ado-
lescence; the secret also which pierces with such
sweetness that when, in very intimate conversation,
the mention of it becomes imminent, we grow awkward and affect to laugh at ourselves; the secret we
cannot hide and cannot tell, though we desire to
do both. We cannot tell it because it is a desire for

something that has never actually appeared in our experience. We cannot hide it because our experience is constantly suggesting it, and we betray ourselves like lovers at the mention of a name. Our commonest expedient is to call it beauty and behave as if that had settled the matter. Wordsworth's expedient was to identify it with certain moments in his own past. But all this is a cheat. If Wordsworth had gone back to those moments in the past, he would not have found the thing itself, but only the reminder of it; what he remembered would turn out to be itself a remembering. The books or the music in which we thought the beauty was located will betray us if we trust to them; it was not *in* them, it only came *through* them, and what came through them was longing. These things—the beauty, the memory of our own past—are good images of what we really desire; but if they are mistaken for the thing itself, they turn into dumb idols, breaking the hearts of their worshippers. For they are not the thing itself; they are only the scent of a flower we have not found, the echo of a tune we have not heard, news from a country we have never yet visited. Do you think I am trying to weave a spell? Perhaps I am; but remember your fairy tales. Spells are used for breaking enchantments as well as for inducing them. And you and I have need of the strongest spell that can be found to wake us from the evil enchantment of worldliness which has been laid upon us for nearly a hundred years. Almost our whole education has been directed to silencing this shy, persistent, inner voice; almost all our modern philosophies have been devised to convince us that the good of man is to be found on this earth. And yet it is a remarkable thing that such philosophies of Progress or Creative Evolution themselves bear reluctant witness to the truth that our real goal is elsewhere. When they want to convince you that earth is your home, notice how they set about it. They begin by trying to persuade you that earth can be made into heaven, thus giving a sop to your sense of exile in earth as it is. Next, they tell you that this fortunate event is still a good way off in the future, thus giving a sop to your knowledge that the fatherland is not here and now. Finally, lest your longing for the transtemporal should awake and spoil the whole affair, they use any rhetoric that comes to hand to keep out of your mind the recollection that even if all the happiness they promised could come to man on earth, yet still each generation would lose it by death, including the last generation of all, and the whole story would be nothing, not even a story, for ever and ever. Hence all the nonsense that Mr. Shaw puts into the final speech of Lilith, and Bergson's remark that the *élan vital* is capable of surmounting all obstacles, perhaps even death—as if we could believe that any social or biological development on this planet will delay the senility of the sun or reverse the second law of thermodynamics.

Do what they will, then, we remain conscious of a desire which no natural happiness will satisfy. But is there any reason to suppose that reality offers any satisfaction to it? "Nor does the being hungry prove that we have bread." But I think it may be urged that this misses the point. A man's physical hunger does not prove that man will get any bread; he may die of starvation on a raft in the Atlantic. But surely a man's hunger does prove that he comes of a race which repairs its body by eating and inhabits a world where eatable substances exist. In the same way, though I do not believe (I wish I did) that my desire for Paradise proves that I shall enjoy it, I think it a pretty good indication that such a thing exists and that some men will. A man may love a woman and not win her; but it would be very odd if the phenomenon called "falling in love" occurred in a sexless world.

Here, then, is the desire, still wandering and uncertain of its object and still largely unable to see that object in the direction where it really lies. Our sacred books give us some account of the object. It is, of course, a symbolical account. Heaven is, by definition, outside our experience, but all intelligible descriptions must be of things within our experience. The scriptural picture of heaven is therefore just as symbolical as the picture which our desire, unaided, invents for itself; heaven is not really full of jewellery any more than it is really the beauty of Nature, or a fine piece of music. The difference is that the scriptural imagery has authority. It comes to us from writers who were closer to God than we, and it has stood the test of Christian experience down the centuries. The natural appeal of this authoritative imagery is to me, at first, very small. At first sight it chills, rather than awakes, my desire. And that is just what I ought to expect. If Christianity could tell me no more of the far-off land than my own temperament led me to surmise already, then Christianity would be no higher than myself. If it has more to give me, I expect it to be less immediately attractive than "my own stuff." Sophocles at first seems dull and cold to the boy who has only reached Shelley. If our religion is something objective, then we must never avert our

eyes from those elements in it which seem puzzling
or repellent; for it will be precisely the puzzling or
the repellent which conceals what we do not yet
know and need to know.

The promises of Scripture may very roughly be
reduced to five heads. It is promised (1) that we
shall be with Christ; (2) that we shall be like Him;
(3) with an enormous wealth of imagery, that we
shall have "glory"; (4) that we shall, in some sense,
be fed or feasted or entertained; and (5) that we
shall have some sort of official position in the universe—ruling cities, judging angels, being pillars
of God's temple. The first question I ask about
these promises is "Why any one of them except the
first?" Can anything be added to the conception of
being with Christ? For it must be true, as an old
writer says, that he who has God and everything
else has no more than he who has God only. I think
the answer turns again on the nature of symbols.
For though it may escape our notice at first glance,
yet it is true that any conception of being with
Christ which most of us can now form will be not
very much less symbolical than the other promises;
for it will smuggle in ideas of proximity in space
and loving conversation as we now understand conversation, and it will probably concentrate on the
humanity of Christ to the exclusion of His deity.
And, in fact, we find that those Christians who
attend solely to this first promise always do fill it
up with very earthly imagery indeed—in fact, with
hymeneal or erotic imagery. I am not for a moment
condemning such imagery. I heartily wish I could
enter into it more deeply than I do, and pray that
I yet shall. But my point is that this also is only a
symbol, like the reality in some respects, but unlike

it in others, and therefore needs correction from the different symbols in the other promises. The variation of the promises does not mean that anything other than God will be our ultimate bliss; but because God is more than a Person, and lest we should imagine the joy of His presence too exclusively in terms of our present poor experience of personal love, with all its narrowness and strain and monotony, a dozen changing images, correcting and relieving each other, are supplied.

I turn next to the idea of glory. There is no getting away from the fact that this idea is very prominent in the New Testament and in early Christian writings. Salvation is constantly associated with palms, crowns, white robes, thrones, and splendour like the sun and stars. All this makes no immediate appeal to me at all, and in that respect I fancy I am a typical modern. Glory suggests two ideas to me, of which one seems wicked and the other ridiculous. Either glory means to me fame, or it means luminosity. As for the first, since to be famous means to be better known than other people, the desire for fame appears to me as a competitive passion and therefore of hell rather than heaven. As for the second, who wishes to become a kind of living electric light bulb?

When I began to look into this matter I was shocked to find such different Christians as Milton, Johnson, and Thomas Aquinas taking heavenly glory quite frankly in the sense of fame or good report. But not fame conferred by our fellow creatures—fame with God, approval or (I might say) "appreciation" by God. And then, when I had thought it over, I saw that this view was scriptural; nothing can eliminate from the parable the divine *accolade,* "Well done, thou good and faithful servant." With that, a good deal of what I had been thinking all my life fell down like a house of cards. I suddenly remembered that no one can enter heaven except as a child; and nothing is so obvious in a child—not in a conceited child, but in a good child—as its great and undisguised pleasure in being praised. Not only in a child, either, but even in a dog or a horse. Apparently what I had mistaken for humility had, all these years, prevented me from understanding what is in fact the humblest, the most childlike, the most creaturely of pleasures—nay, the specific pleasure of the inferior: the pleasure of a beast before men, a child before its father, a pupil before his teacher, a creature before its Creator. I am not forgetting how horribly this most innocent desire is parodied in our human ambitions, or how very quickly, in my own experience, the lawful pleasure of praise from those whom it was my duty to please turns into the deadly poison of self-admiration. But I thought I could detect a moment—a very, very short moment—before this happened, during which the satisfaction of having pleased those whom I rightly loved and rightly feared was pure. And that is enough to raise our thoughts to what may happen when the redeemed soul, beyond all hope and nearly beyond belief, learns at last that she has pleased Him whom she was created to please. There will be no room for vanity then. She will be free from the miserable illusion that it is her doing. With no taint of what we should now call self-approval she will most innocently rejoice in the thing that God has made her to be, and the moment which heals her old inferiority complex forever will also drown her pride deeper than Prospero's book. Perfect humility dispenses with modesty. If God is satisfied with the work, the work may be satisfied with itself; "it is not for her to bandy compliments with her Sovereign." I can imagine someone saying that he dislikes my idea of heaven as a place where we are patted on the back. But proud misunderstanding is behind that dislike. In the end that Face which is the delight or the terror of the universe must be turned upon each of us either with one expression or with the other, either conferring glory inexpressible or inflicting shame that can never be cured or disguised. I read in a periodical the other day that the fundamental thing is how we think of God. By God Himself, it is not! How God thinks of us is not only more important, but infinitely more important. Indeed, how we think of Him is of no importance except insofar as it is related to how He thinks of us. It is written that we shall "stand before" Him, shall appear, shall be inspected. The promise of glory is the promise, almost incredible and only possible by the work of Christ, that some of us, that any of us who really chooses, shall actually survive that examination, shall find approval, shall please God. To please God . . . to be a real ingredient in the divine happiness . . . to be loved by God, not merely pitied, but delighted in as an artist delights in his work or a father in a son —it seems impossible, a weight or burden of glory which our thoughts can hardly sustain. But so it is.

And now notice what is happening. If I had rejected the authoritative and scriptural image of glory and stuck obstinately to the vague desire which was, at the outset, my only pointer to heaven, I could have seen no connection at all between that desire and the Christian promise. But now, having followed up what seemed puzzling and repellent in the sacred books, I find, to my great surprise, looking back, that the connection is perfectly clear. Glory, as Christianity teaches me to hope for it, turns out to satisfy my original desire and indeed to reveal an element in that desire which I had not noticed. By ceasing for a moment to consider my own wants I have begun to learn better what I really wanted. When I attempted, a few minutes ago, to describe our spiritual longings, I was omitting one of their most curious characteristics. We usually notice it just as the moment of vision dies away, as the music ends, or as the landscape loses the celestial light. What we feel then has been well described by Keats as "the journey homeward to habitual self." You know what I mean. For a few minutes we have had the illusion of belonging to that world. Now we wake to find that it is no such thing. We have been mere spectators. Beauty has smiled, but not to welcome us; her face was turned in our direction, but not to see us. We have not been accepted, welcomed, or taken into the dance. We may go when we please, we may stay if we can: "Nobody marks us." A scientist may reply that since most of the things we call beautiful are inanimate, it is not very surprising that they take no notice of us. That, of course, is true. It is not the physical objects that I am speaking of, but that indescribable something of which they become for a moment the messengers. And part of the bitterness which mixes with the sweetness of that message is due to the fact that it so seldom seems to be a message intended for us, but rather something we have overheard. By bitterness I mean pain, not resentment. We should hardly dare to ask that any notice be taken of ourselves. But we pine. The sense that in this universe we are treated as strangers, the longing to be acknowledged, to meet with some response, to bridge some chasm that yawns between us and reality, is part of our inconsolable secret. And surely, from this point of view, the promise of glory, in the sense described, becomes highly relevant to our deep desire. For glory means good report with God, acceptance by God, response, acknowledgement, and welcome into the heart of things. The door on which we have been knocking all our lives will open at last.

Perhaps it seems rather crude to describe glory as the fact of being "noticed" by God. But this is almost the language of the New Testament. St. Paul promises to those who love God not, as we should expect, that they will know Him, but that they will be known by Him (1 Cor. 8:3). It is a strange promise. Does not God know all things at all times? But it is dreadfully re-echoed in another passage of the New Testament. There we are warned that it may happen to anyone of us to appear at last before the face of God and hear only the appalling words, "I never knew you. Depart from Me." In some sense, as dark to the intellect as it is unendurable to the feelings, we can be both banished from the presence of Him who is present everywhere and erased from the knowledge of Him who knows all. We can be left utterly and absolutely *outside* —repelled, exiled, estranged, finally and unspeakably ignored. On the other hand, we can be called in, welcomed, received, acknowledged. We walk every day on the razor edge between these two incredible possibilities. Apparently, then, our life-long nostalgia, our longing to be reunited with something in the universe from which we now feel cut off, to be on the inside of some door which we have always seen from the outside, is no mere neurotic fancy, but the truest index of our real situation. And to be at last summoned inside would be both glory and honour beyond all our merits and also the healing of that old ache.

And this brings me to the other sense of glory—glory as brightness, splendour, luminosity. We are to shine as the sun, we are to be given the Morning Star. I think I begin to see what it means. In one way, of course, God has given us the Morning Star already: you can go and enjoy the gift on many fine mornings if you get up early enough. What more, you may ask, do we want? Ah, but we want so much more—something the books on aesthetics take little notice of. But the poets and the mythologies know all about it. We do not want merely to *see* beauty, though, God knows, even that is bounty enough. We want something else which can hardly be put into words—to be united with the beauty we see, to pass into it, to receive it into ourselves, to bathe in it, to become part of it. That is why we have peopled air and earth and water with gods and goddesses and nymphs and elves—that, though we cannot, yet these projections can enjoy in themselves that beauty, grace, and power of which Nature is the image. That is why the poets tell us such lovely falsehoods. They talk as if the west wind could really sweep into a human soul; but it can't. They tell us that "beauty born of murmuring sound" will pass into a human face; but it won't. Or not yet. For if we take the imagery of Scripture seriously, if we believe that God will one day *give* us the Morning Star and cause us to *put on* the splendour of the sun, then we may surmise that both the ancient myths and the modern poetry, so false as history, may be very near the truth as prophecy. At present we are on the outside of the world, the wrong side of the door. We discern the freshness and purity of morning, but they do not make us fresh and pure. We cannot mingle with the splendours we see. But all the leaves of the New Testament are rustling with the rumour that it will not always be so. Some day, God willing, we shall get *in*. When human souls have become as perfect in voluntary obedience as the inanimate creation is in its lifeless obedience, then they will put on its glory, or rather that greater glory of which Nature is only the first sketch. For you must not think that I am putting forward any heathen fancy of being absorbed into Nature. Nature is mortal; we shall outlive her. When all the suns and nebulae have passed away, each one of you will still be alive. Nature is only the image, the symbol; but it is the symbol Scripture invites me to use. We are summoned to pass in through Nature, beyond her, into that splendour which she fitfully reflects.

And in there, in beyond Nature, we shall eat of the tree of life. At present, if we are reborn in Christ, the spirit in us lives directly on God; but the mind and, still more, the body receives life from Him at a thousand removes—through our ancestors, through our food, through the elements. The faint, far-off results of those energies which God's creative rapture implanted in matter when He made the worlds are what we now call physical pleasures; and even thus filtered, they are too much for our present management. What would it be to taste at the fountainhead that stream of which even these lower reaches prove so intoxicating? Yet that, I believe, is what lies before us. The whole man is to drink joy from the fountain of joy. As St. Augustine said, the rapture of the saved soul will "flow over" into the glorified body. In the light of our present specialised and depraved appetites, we cannot imagine this *torrens voluptatis*, and I warn everyone most seriously not to try. But it must be mentioned, to drive out thoughts even more misleading—thoughts that what is saved is a mere ghost, or that the risen body lives in numb insensibility. The body was made for the Lord, and these dismal fancies are wide of the mark.

Meanwhile the cross comes before the crown and tomorrow is a Monday morning. A cleft has opened in the pitiless walls of the world, and we are invited to follow our great Captain inside. The following Him is, of course, the essential point. That being so, it may be asked what practical use there is in the speculations which I have been indulging. I can think of at least one such use. It may be possible for each to think too much of his own potential glory hereafter; it is hardly possible for him to think too often or too deeply about that of his neighbour. The load, or weight, or burden of my neighbour's glory should be laid on my back, a load so heavy that only humility can carry it, and the backs of the proud will be broken. It is a serious thing to live in a society of possible gods and goddesses, to remember that the dullest and most uninteresting person you can talk to may one day be a creature which, if you say it now, you would be strongly tempted to worship, or else a horror and a corruption such as you now meet, if at all, only in a nightmare. All day long we are, in some degree, helping each other to one or other of these destinations. It is in the light of these overwhelming possibilities, it is with the awe and the circumspection proper to them, that we should conduct all our dealings with one another, all friendships, all loves, all play, all politics. There are no *ordinary* people. You have never talked to a mere mortal. Nations, cultures, arts, civilisations—these are mortal, and their life is to ours as the life of a gnat. But it is immortals whom we joke with, work with, marry, snub, and exploit—immortal horrors or everlasting splendours. This does not mean that we are to be perpetually solemn. We must play. But our merriment must be of that kind (and it is, in fact, the merriest kind) which exists between people who have, from the outset, taken each other seriously—no flippancy, no superiority, no presumption. And our charity must be a real and costly love, with deep feeling for the sins in spite of which we love the sinner—no mere tolerance, or indulgence which parodies love as flippancy parodies merriment. Next to the Blessed Sacrament itself, your neighbour is the holiest object presented to your senses. If he is your Christian neighbour, he is holy in almost the same way, for in him also Christ *vere latitat*—the glorifier and the glorified, Glory Himself, is truly hidden.

LEARNING
IN WAR-TIME

A university is a society for the pursuit of learning. As students, you will be expected to make yourselves, or to start making yourselves, into what the Middle Ages called clerks: into philosophers, scientists, scholars, critics, or historians. And at first sight this seems to be an odd thing to do during a great war. What is the use of beginning a task which we have so little chance of finishing? Or, even if we ourselves should happen not to be interrupted by death or military service, why should we—indeed how can we—continue to take an interest in these placid occupations when the lives of our friends and the liberties of Europe are in the balance? Is it not like fiddling while Rome burns?

Now it seems to me that we shall not be able to answer these questions until we have put them by the side of certain other questions which every Christian ought to have asked himself in peacetime. I spoke just now of fiddling while Rome burns. But to a Christian the true tragedy of Nero must be not that he fiddled while the city was on fire but that he fiddled on the brink of hell. You must forgive me for the crude monosyllable. I know that many wiser and better Christians than I in these days do not like to mention Heaven and hell even in a pulpit. I know, too, that nearly all the references to this subject in the New Testament come from a single source. But then that source is Our Lord

Himself. People will tell you it is St. Paul, but that is untrue. These overwhelming doctrines are dominical. They are not really removable from the teaching of Christ or of His Church. If we do not believe them, our presence in this church is great tomfoolery. If we do, we must sometime overcome our spiritual prudery and mention them.

The moment we do so we can see that every Christian who comes to a university must at all times face a question compared with which the questions raised by the war are relatively unimportant. He must ask himself how it is right, or even psychologically possible, for creatures who are every moment advancing either to Heaven or to hell to spend any fraction of the little time allowed them in this world on such comparative trivialities as literature or art, mathematics or biology. If human culture can stand up to that, it can stand up to anything. To admit that we can retain our interest in learning under the shadow of these eternal issues but not under the shadow of a European war would be to admit that our ears are closed to the voice of reason and very wide open to the voice of our nerves and our mass emotions.

This indeed is the case with most of us, certainly with me. For this reason I think it important to try to see the present calamity in a true perspective. The war creates no absolutely new situation; it simply aggravates the permanent human situation so that we can no longer ignore it. Human life has always been lived on the edge of a precipice. Human culture has always had to exist under the shadow of something infinitely more important than itself. If men had postponed the search for knowledge and beauty until they were secure, the search would never have begun. We are mistaken when we compare war with "normal life." Life has never been normal. Even those periods which we think most tranquil, like the nineteenth century, turn out, on closer inspection, to be full of crises, alarms, difficulties, emergencies. Plausible reasons have never been lacking for putting off all merely cultural activities until some imminent danger has been averted or some crying injustice put right. But humanity long ago chose to neglect those plausible reasons. They wanted knowledge and beauty now, and would not wait for the suitable moment that never comes. Periclean Athens leaves us not only the Parthenon but, significantly, the Funeral Oration. The insects have chosen a different line: they have sought first the material welfare and security of the hive, and presumably they have their reward. Men are different. They propound mathematical theorems in beleaguered cities, conduct metaphysical arguments in condemned cells, make jokes on scaffolds, discuss the last new poem while advancing to the walls of Quebec, and comb their hair at Thermopylae. This is not *panache*; it is our nature.

But since we are fallen creatures, the fact that this is now our nature would not, by itself, prove that it is rational or right. We have to inquire whether there is really any legitimate place for the activities of the scholar in a world such as this. That is, we have always to answer the question, "How can you be so frivolous and selfish as to think about anything but the salvation of human souls?" and we have, at the moment, to answer the additional question, "How can you be so frivolous and selfish as to think of anything but the war?" Now part of our answer will be the same for both questions. The

one implies that our life can, and ought, to become
exclusively and explicitly religious, the other, that
it can and ought to become exclusively national.
I believe that our whole life can, and indeed must,
become religious in a sense to be explained later.
But if it is meant that all our activities are to be of
the kind that can be recognised as "sacred" as
opposed to "secular," then I would give a single
reply to both my imaginary assailants. I would say,
"Whether it ought to happen or not, the thing you
are recommending is not going to happen." Before
I became a Christian I do not think I fully realised
that one's life, after conversion, would inevitably
consist in doing most of the same things one had
been doing before, one hopes, in a new spirit, but
still the same things. Before I went to the last war
I certainly expected that my life in the trenches
would, in some mysterious sense, be all war. In fact,
I found that the nearer you got to the front line the
less everyone spoke and thought of the allied cause
and the progress of the campaign; and I am pleased
to find that Tolstoi, in the greatest war book ever
written, records the same thing—and so, in its own
way, does the *Iliad*. Neither conversion nor enlist-
ment in the army is really going to obliterate our
human life. Christians and soldiers are still men;
the infidel's idea of a religious life and the civilian's
idea of active service are fantastic. If you attempted,
in either case, to suspend your whole intellectual
and aesthetic activity, you would only succeed in
substituting a worse cultural life for a better. You
are not, in fact, going to read nothing, either in the
Church or in the line; if you don't read good books,
you will read bad ones. If you don't go on thinking
rationally, you will think irrationally. If you reject

aesthetic satisfactions, you will fall into sensual satisfactions.

There is therefore this analogy between the claims of our religion and the claims of the war: neither of them, for most of us, will simply cancel or remove from the slate the merely human life which we were leading before we entered them. But they will operate in this way for different reasons. The war will fail to absorb our whole attention because it is a finite object and, therefore, intrinsically unfitted to support the whole attention of a human soul. In order to avoid misunderstanding I must here make a few distinctions. I believe our cause to be, as human causes go, very righteous, and I therefore believe it to be a duty to participate in this war. And every duty is a religious duty, and our obligation to perform every duty is therefore absolute. Thus we may have a duty to rescue a drowning man and, perhaps, if we live on a dangerous coast, to learn lifesaving so as to be ready for any drowning man when he turns up. It may be our duty to lose our own lives in saving him. But if anyone devoted himself to lifesaving in the sense of giving it his total attention—so that he thought and spoke of nothing else and demanded the cessation of all other human activities until everyone had learned to swim—he would be a monomaniac. The rescue of drowning men is, then, a duty worth dying for, but not worth living for. It seems to me that all political duties (among which I include military duties) are of this kind. A man may have to die for our country, but no man must, in any exclusive sense, live for his country. He who surrenders himself without reservation to the temporal claims of a nation, or a party, or a class is rendering to Caesar that which, of all things, most emphatically belongs to God: himself.

It is for a very different reason that religion cannot occupy the whole of life in the sense of excluding all our natural activities. For, of course, in some sense, it must occupy the whole of life. There is no question of a compromise between the claims of God and the claims of culture, or politics, or anything else. God's claim is infinite and inexorable. You can refuse it, or you can begin to try to grant it. There is no middle way. Yet in spite of this it is clear that Christianity does not exclude any of the ordinary human activities. St. Paul tells people to get on with their jobs. He even assumes that Christians may go to dinner parties, and, what is more, dinner parties given by pagans. Our Lord attends a wedding and provides miraculous wine. Under the aegis of His Church, and in the most Christian ages, learning and the arts flourish. The solution of this paradox is, of course, well known to you. "Whether ye eat or drink or whatsoever ye do, do all to the glory of God."

All our merely natural activities will be accepted, if they are offered to God, even the humblest, and all of them, even the noblest, will be sinful if they are not. Christianity does not simply replace our natural life and substitute a new one; it is rather a new organisation which exploits, to its own supernatural ends, these natural materials. No doubt, in a given situation, it demands the surrender of some, or of all, our merely human pursuits; it is better to be saved with one eye, than, having two, to be cast into Gehenna. But it does this, in a sense, *per accidens*—because, in those special circumstances, it has ceased to be possible to practise this or that activity to the glory of God. There is no essential quarrel between the spiritual life and the human activities as such. Thus the omnipresence of obedience to God in a Christian's life is, in a way, analogous to the omnipresence of God in space. God does not fill space as a body fills it, in the sense that parts of Him are in different parts of space, excluding other objects from them. Yet He is everywhere—totally present at every point of space—according to good theologians.

We are now in a position to answer the view that human culture is an inexcusable frivolity on the part of creatures loaded with such awful responsibilities as we. I reject at once an idea which lingers in the mind of some modern people that cultural activities are in their own right spiritual and meritorious—as though scholars and poets were intrinsically more pleasing to God than scavengers and bootblacks. I think it was Matthew Arnold who first used the English word *spiritual* in the sense of the German *geistlich*, and so inaugurated this most dangerous and most anti-Christian error. Let us clear it forever from our minds. The work of a Beethoven and the work of a charwoman become spiritual on precisely the same condition, that of being offered to God, of being done humbly "as to the Lord." This does not, of course, mean that it is for anyone a mere toss-up whether he should sweep rooms or compose symphonies. A mole must dig to the glory of God and a cock must crow. We are members of one body, but differentiated members, each with his own vocation. A man's upbringing, his talents, his circumstances, are usually a tolerable index of his vocation. If our parents have sent us to Oxford, if our country allows us to remain there, this is *prima facie* evidence that the life which we, at any rate, can best lead to the glory of God at present is the learned life. By leading that life to the glory of God I do not, of course, mean any attempt to make our intellectual inquiries work out to edifying conclusions. That would be, as Bacon says, to offer to the author of truth the unclean sacrifice of a lie. I mean the pursuit of knowledge and beauty, in a sense, for their own sake, but in a sense which does not exclude their being for God's sake. An appetite for these things exists in the human mind, and God makes no appetite in vain. We can therefore pursue knowledge as such, and beauty as such, in the sure confidence that by so doing we are either advancing to the vision of God ourselves or indirectly helping others to do so. Humility, no less than the appetite, encourages us to concentrate simply on the knowledge or the beauty, not too much concerning ourselves with their ultimate relevance to the vision of God. That relevance may not be intended for us but for our betters—for men who come after and find the spiritual significance of what we dug out in blind and humble obedience to our vocation. This is the teleological argument that the existence of the impulse and the faculty prove that they must have a proper function in God's scheme—the argument by which Thomas Aquinas proves that sexuality would have existed even without the Fall. The soundness of the argument, as regards culture, is proved by experience. The intellectual life is not the only road to God, nor the safest, but we find it to be a road, and it may be the appointed road for us. Of course, it will be so only so long as we keep the impulse pure and disinterested. That is the great difficulty.

As the author of the *Theologia Germanica* says, we may come to love knowledge—*our* knowing—more than the thing known: to delight not in the exercise of our talents but in the fact that they are ours, or even in the reputation they bring us. Every success in the scholar's life increases this danger. If it becomes irresistible, he must give up his scholarly work. The time for plucking out the right eye has arrived.

That is the essential nature of the learned life as I see it. But it has indirect values which are especially important today. If all the world were Christian, it might not matter if all the world were uneducated. But, as it is, a cultural life will exist outside the Church whether it exists inside or not. To be ignorant and simple now—not to be able to meet the enemies on their own ground—would be to throw down our weapons, and to betray our uneducated brethren who have, under God, no defence but us against the intellectual attacks of the heathen. Good philosophy must exist, if for no other reason, because bad philosophy needs to be answered. The cool intellect must work not only against cool intellect on the other side, but against the muddy heathen mysticisms which deny intellect altogether. Most of all, perhaps, we need intimate knowledge of the past. Not that the past has any magic about it, but because we cannot study the future, and yet need something to set against the present, to remind us that the basic assumptions have been quite different in different periods and that much which seems certain to the uneducated is merely temporary fashion. A man who has lived in many places is not likely to be deceived by the local errors of his native village; the scholar has lived in many times and is therefore in some degree immune from the great cataract of nonsense that pours from the press and the microphone of his own age.

The learned life then is, for some, a duty. At the moment it looks as if it were your duty. I am well aware that there may seem to be an almost comic discrepancy between the high issues we have been considering and the immediate task you may be set down to, such as Anglo-Saxon sound laws or chemical formulae. But there is a similar shock awaiting us in every vocation—a young priest finds himself involved in choir treats and a young sub-altern in accounting for pots of jam. It is well that it should be so. It weeds out the vain, windy people and keeps in those who are both humble and tough. On that kind of difficulty we need waste no sympathy. But the peculiar difficulty imposed on you by the war is another matter, and of it I would again repeat what I have been saying in one form or another ever since I started—do not let your nerves and emotions lead you into thinking your predicament more abnormal than it really is. Perhaps it may be useful to mention the three mental exercises which may serve as defences against the three enemies which war raises up against the scholar.

The first enemy is excitement—the tendency to think and feel about the war when we had intended to think about our work. The best defence is a recognition that in this, as in everything else, the war has not really raised up a new enemy but only aggravated an old one. There are always plenty of rivals to our work. We are always falling in love or quarrelling, looking for jobs or fearing to lose them, getting ill and recovering, following public affairs. If we let ourselves, we shall always be waiting for some distraction or other to end before we can really get down to our work. The only people who achieve much are those who want knowledge so badly that they seek it while the conditions are still unfavourable. Favourable conditions never come. There are, of course, moments when the pressure of the excitement is so great that only superhuman self-control could resist it. They come both in war and peace. We must do the best we can.

The second enemy is frustration—the feeling that we shall not have time to finish. If I say to you that no one has time to finish, that the longest human life leaves a man, in any branch of learning, a beginner, I shall seem to you to be saying something quite academic and theoretical. You would be surprised if you knew how soon one begins to feel the shortness of the tether, of how many things, even in middle life, we have to say "No time for that," "Too late now," and "Not for me." But Nature herself forbids you to share that experience. A more Christian attitude, which can be attained at any age, is that of leaving futurity in God's hands. We may as well, for God will certainly retain it whether we leave it to Him or not. Never, in peace or war, commit your virtue or your happiness to the future. Happy work is best done by the man who takes his long-term plans somewhat lightly and works from moment to moment "as to the Lord." It is only our *daily* bread that we are encouraged to ask for. The present is the only time in which any duty can be done or any grace received.

The third enemy is fear. War threatens us with death and pain. No man—and specially no Christian who remembers Gethsemane—need try to attain a stoic indifference about these things, but we can guard against the illusions of the imagination. We think of the streets of Warsaw and contrast the deaths there suffered with an abstraction called Life. But there is no question of death or life for any of us, only a question of this death or of that—of a machine gun bullet now or a cancer forty years later. What does war do to death? It certainly does not make it more frequent; 100 per cent of us die, and the percentage cannot be increased. It puts several deaths earlier, but I hardly suppose that that is what we fear. Certainly when the moment comes, it will make little difference how many years we have behind us. Does it increase our chances of a painful death? I doubt it. As far as I can find out, what we call natural death is usually preceded by suffering, and a battlefield is one of the very few places where one has a reasonable prospect of dying with no pain at all. Does it decrease our chances of dying at peace with God? I cannot believe it. If active service does not persuade a man to prepare for death, what conceivable concatenation of circumstances would? Yet war does do something to death. It forces us to remember it. The only reason why the cancer at sixty or the paralysis at seventy-five do not bother us is that we forget them. War makes death real to us, and that would have been regarded as one of its blessings by most of the great Christians of the past. They thought it good for us to be always aware of our mortality. I am inclined to think they were right. All the animal life in us, all schemes of happiness that centred in this world, were always doomed to a final frustration. In ordinary times only a wise man can realise it. Now the stupidest of us knows. We see unmistakably the sort of universe in which we have all along been living, and must come to terms with it. If we had foolish un-Christian hopes about human culture, they are now shattered. If we thought we were building up a heaven on earth, if we looked for something that would turn the present world from a place of pilgrimage into a permanent city satisfying the soul of man, we are disillusioned, and not a moment too soon. But if we thought that for some souls, and at some times, the life of learning, humbly offered to God, was, in its own small way, one of the appointed approaches to the Divine reality and the Divine beauty which we hope to enjoy hereafter, we can think so still.

WHY I AM NOT
A PACIFIST

The question is whether to serve in the wars at the command of the civil society to which we belong is a wicked action, or an action morally indifferent, or an action morally obligatory. In asking how to decide this question, we are raising a much more general question: how do we decide what is good or evil? The usual answer is that we decide by conscience. But probably no one thinks now of conscience as a separate faculty, like one of the senses. Indeed, it cannot be so thought of. For an autonomous faculty like a sense cannot be argued with; you cannot argue a man into seeing green if he sees blue. But the conscience can be altered by argument; and if you did not think so, you would not have asked me to come and argue with you about the morality of obeying the civil law when it tells us to serve in the wars. Conscience, then, means the whole man engaged in a particular subject matter.

But even in this sense conscience still has two meanings. It can mean (a) the pressure a man feels upon his will to do what he thinks is right; (b) his judgment as to what the content of right and wrong are. In sense (a) conscience is always to be followed. It is the sovereign of the universe, which "if it had power as it has right, would absolutely rule the world." It is not to be argued with, but obeyed, and even to question it is to incur guilt. But in sense

(b) it is a very different matter. People may be mistaken about wrong and right; most people in some degree are mistaken. By what means are mistakes in this field to be corrected?

The most useful analogy here is that of Reason— by which I do not mean some separate faculty but, once more, the whole man judging, only judging this time not about good and evil, but about truth and falsehood. Now any concrete train of reasoning involves three elements: *Firstly*, there is the reception of facts to reason about. These facts are received either from our own senses, or from the report of other minds; that is, either experience or authority supplies us with our material. But each man's experience is so limited that the second source is the more usual; of every hundred facts upon which to reason, ninety-nine depend on authority. *Secondly*, there is the direct, simple act of the mind perceiving self-evident truth, as when we see that if A and B both equal C, then they equal each other. This act I call intuition. *Thirdly*, there is an art or skill of arranging the facts so as to yield a series of such intuitions which linked together produce a proof of the truth or falsehood of the proposition we are considering. Thus in a geometrical proof each step is seen by intuition, and to fail to see it is to be not a bad geometrician but an idiot. The skill comes in arranging the material into a series of intuitable "steps." Failure to do this does not mean idiocy, but only lack of ingenuity or invention. Failure to follow it need not mean idiocy, but either inattention or a defect of memory which forbids us to hold all the intuitions together.

Now all correction of errors in reasoning is really correction of the first or the third element. The second, the intuitional element, cannot be corrected if it is wrong, nor supplied if it is lacking. You can give the man new facts. You can invent a simpler proof, that is, a simpler concatenation of intuitable truths. But when you come to an absolute inability to see any one of the self-evident steps out of which the proof is built, then you can do nothing. No doubt this absolute inability is much rarer than we suppose. Every teacher knows that people are constantly protesting that they "can't see" some self-evident inference, but the supposed inability is usually a refusal to see, resulting either from some passion which *wants* not to see the truth in question or else from sloth which does not want to think at all. But when the inability is real, argument is at an end. You cannot produce rational intuition by argument, because argument depends upon rational intuition. Proof rests upon the unprovable which has to be just "seen." Hence faulty intuition is incorrigible. It does not follow that it cannot be trained by practice in attention and in the mortification of disturbing passions, or corrupted by the opposite habits. But it is not amenable to correction by argument.

Before leaving the subject of Reason, I must point out that authority not only combines with experience to produce the raw material, the "facts," but also has to be frequently used instead of reasoning itself as a method of getting conclusions. For example, few of us have followed the reasoning on which even ten percent of the truths we believe are based. We accept them on authority from the experts and are wise to do so, for though we are thereby sometimes deceived, yet we should have to live like savages if we did not.

Now all three elements are found also in conscience. The facts, as before, come from experience and authority. I do not mean "moral facts" but those facts about actions without holding which we could not raise moral questions at all—for we should not even be discussing Pacifism if we did not know what war and killing meant, nor Chastity, if we had not yet learned what schoolmasters used to call "the facts of life." Secondly, there are the pure intuitions of utterly simple good and evil as such. Third, there is the process of argument by which you arrange the intuitions so as to convince a man that a particular act is wrong or right. And finally, there is authority as a substitute for argument, telling a man of some wrong or right which he would not otherwise have discovered, and rightly accepted if the man has good reason to believe the authority wiser and better than himself. The main difference between Reason and Conscience is an alarming one. It is thus: that while the unarguable intuitions on which all depend are liable to be corrupted by passion when we are considering truth and falsehood, they are much more liable, they are almost certain to be corrupted when we are considering good and evil. For then we are concerned with some action to be here and now done or left undone by ourselves. And we should not be considering that action at all unless we had some wish either to do or not to do it, so that in this sphere we are bribed from the very beginning. Hence the value of authority in checking, or even superseding, our own activity is much greater in this sphere than in that of Reason. Hence, too, human beings must be trained in obedience to the moral intuitions almost before they have them, and years before they are rational enough to discuss them, or they will be corrupted before the time for discussion arrives.

These basic moral intuitions are the only element in Conscience which cannot be argued about; if there can be a difference of opinion which does not reveal one of the parties as a moral idiot, then it is not an intuition. They are the ultimate preferences of the will for love rather than hatred and happiness rather than misery. There are people so corrupted as to have lost even these, just as there are people who can't see the simplest proof, but in the main these can be said to be the voice of humanity as such. And they are unarguable. But here the trouble begins. People are constantly claiming this unarguable and unanswerable status for moral judgments which are not really intuitions at all but remote consequences or particular applications of them, eminently open to discussion since the consequences may be illogically drawn or the application falsely made.

Thus you may meet a "temperance" fanatic who claims to have an unanswerable intuition that all strong drink is forbidden. Really he can have nothing of the sort. The real intuition is that health and harmony are good. Then there is a generalisation from facts to the effect that drunkenness produces disease and quarrelling, and perhaps also, if the fanatic is Christian, the voice of Authority saying that the body is the temple of the Holy Ghost. Then there is a conclusion that what can always be abused had better never be used at all—a conclusion eminently suited for discussion. Finally, there is the process whereby early associations, arrogance, and the like turn the remote conclusion into something which the man thinks unarguable because he does not wish to argue about it.

This then, is our first canon for moral decisions. Conscience in the (a) sense, the thing that moves us to do right, has absolute authority, but conscience in the (b) sense, our judgment as to what is right, is a mixture of inarguable intuitions and highly arguable processes of reasoning or of submission to authority; and nothing is to be treated as an intuition unless it is such that no good man has ever dreamed of doubting. The man who "just feels" that total abstinence from drink or marriage is obligatory is to be treated like the man who "just feels sure" that *Henry VIII* is not by Shakespeare or that vaccination does no good. For a mere unargued conviction is in place only when we are dealing with the axiomatic; and these views are not axiomatic.

I therefore begin by ruling out one Pacifist position which probably no one present holds, but which conceivably might be held—that of the man who claims to know on the ground of immediate intuition that all killing of human beings is in all circumstances an absolute evil. With the man who reaches the same result by reasoning or authority, I can argue. Of the man who claims not to reach it but to start there, we can only say that he can have no such intuition as he claims. He is mistaking an opinion, or, more likely, a passion, for an intuition. Of course, it would be rude to say this to him. *To* him we can only say that if he is not a moral idiot, then unfortunately the rest of the human race, including its best and wisest, are, and that argument across such a chasm is impossible.

Having ruled out this extreme case, I return to

enquire how we are to decide on a question of morals. We have seen that every moral judgment involves facts, intuition, and reasoning, and, if we are wise enough to be humble, it will involve some regard for authority as well. Its strength depends on the strength of these four factors. Thus if I find that the facts on which I am working are clear and little disputed, that the basic intuition is unmistakably an intuition, that the reasoning which connects this intuition with the particular judgment is strong, and that I am in agreement or (at worst) not in disagreement with authority, then I can trust my moral judgment with reasonable confidence. And if, in addition, I find little reason to suppose that any passion has secretly swayed my mind, this confidence is confirmed. If, on the other hand, I find the facts doubtful, the supposed intuition by no means obvious to all good men, the reasoning weak, and authority against me, then I ought to conclude that I am probably wrong. And if the conclusion which I have reached turns out also to flatter some strong passion of my own, then my suspicion should deepen into moral certainty. By "moral certainty" I mean that degree of certainty proper to moral decisions; for mathematical certainty is not here to be looked for. I now apply these tests to the judgment, "It is immoral to obey when the civil society of which I am a member commands me to serve in the wars!"

First as to the facts. The main relevant fact admitted by all parties is that war is very disagreeable. The main contention urged as fact by pacifists would be that wars always do more harm than good. How is one to find out whether this is true? It belongs to a class of historical generalisations which involve a comparison between the actual consequences of some actual event and a consequence which might have followed if that event had not occurred. "Wars do no good" involves the proposition that if the Greeks had yielded to Xerxes and the Romans to Hannibal, the course of history ever since would have been perhaps better, but certainly no worse than it actually has been; that a Mediterranean world in which Carthaginian power succeeded Persian would have been at least as good and happy and as fruitful for all posterity as the actual Mediterranean world in which Roman power succeeded Greek. My point is not that such an opinion seems to me overwhelmingly improbable. My point is that both opinions are merely speculative; there is no conceivable way of convincing a man of either. Indeed it is doubtful whether the whole conception of "what would have happened"—that is, of unrealised possibilities—is more than an imaginative technique for giving a vivid rhetorical account of what did happen.

That wars do no good is then so far from being a fact that it hardly ranks as a historical opinion. Nor is the matter mended by saying "modern wars"; how are we to decide whether the total effect would have been better or worse if Europe had submitted to Germany in 1914? It is, of course, true that wars never do half the good which the leaders of the belligerents say they are going to do. Nothing ever does half the good—perhaps nothing ever does half the evil—which is expected of it. And that may be a sound argument for not pitching one's propaganda too high. But it is no argument against war. If a Germanised Europe in 1914 would have been an evil, then the war which prevented that evil was, so far, justified. To call it useless because it did not also cure slums and unemployment is like coming up to a man who has just succeeded in defending himself from a man-eating tiger and saying, "It's no good, old chap. This hasn't really cured your rheumatism!"

On the test of fact, then, I find the Pacifist position weak. It seems to me that history is full of useful wars as well as of useless wars. If all that can be brought against the frequent appearance of utility is mere speculation about what would have happened, I am not converted.

I turn next to the intuition. There is no question of discussion once we have found it; there is only the danger of mistaking for an intuition something which is really a conclusion and therefore needs argument. We want something which no good man has ever disputed; we are in search of platitude. The relevant intuition seems to be that love is good and hatred bad, or that helping is good and harming bad.

We have next to consider whether reasoning leads us from this intuition to the Pacifist conclusion or not. And the first thing I notice is that intuition can lead to no action until it is limited in some way or other. You cannot do *simply* good to *simply* Man; you must do this or that good to this or that man. And if you do *this* good, you can't at the same time do that; and if you do it to *these* men, you can't also do it to *those*. Hence from the outset the law of beneficence involves not doing some good to some men at some times. Hence those rules which so far as I know have never been doubted, as that we should help one we have promised to help rather than another, or a benefactor rather than one who has no special claims on us, or a compatriot more than a stranger, or a kinsman rather than a mere compatriot. And this in fact most often means helping A at the expense of B, who drowns while you pull A on board. And sooner or later, it involves helping A by actually doing some degree of violence to B. But when B is up to mischief against A, you must either do nothing (which disobeys the intuition) or you must help one against the other. And certainly no one's conscience tells him to help B, the guilty. It remains, therefore, to help A. So far, I suppose, we all agree. If the argument is not to end in an anti-Pacifist conclusion, one or other of two stopping places must be selected. You must either say that violence to B is lawful only if it stops short of killing, or else that killing of individuals is indeed lawful but the mass killing of a war is not.

As regards the first, I admit the general proposition that the lesser violence done to B is always preferable to the greater, provided that it is equally efficient in restraining him and equally good for everyone concerned, including B, whose claim is inferior to all the other claims involved but not nonexistent. But I do not therefore conclude that to kill B is always wrong. In some instances—for instance in a small, isolated community, death may be the only efficient method of restraint. In any community its effect on the population, not simply as a deterrent through fear, but also as an expression of the moral importance of certain crimes, may be valuable. And as for B himself, I think a bad man is at least as likely to make a good end in the execution shed some weeks after the crime as in the prison hospital twenty years later. I am not producing arguments to show that capital punishment is certainly right; I am only maintaining that it is not certainly wrong; it is a matter on which good men may legitimately differ.

As regards the second, the position seems to be much clearer. It is arguable that a criminal can always be satisfactorily dealt with without the death penalty. It is certain that a whole nation cannot be prevented from taking what it wants except by war. It is almost equally certain that the absorption of certain societies by certain other societies is a great evil. The doctrine that war is always a greater evil seems to imply a materialist ethic, a belief that death and pain are the greatest evils. But I do not think they are. I think the suppression of a higher religion by a lower, or even a higher secular culture by a lower, a much greater evil. Nor am I greatly moved by the fact that many of the individuals we strike down in war are innocent. That seems, in a way, to make war not worse but better. All men die, and most men miserably. That two soldiers on opposite sides, each believing his own country to be in the right, each at the moment when his selfishness is most in abeyance and his will to sacrifice in the ascendant, should kill other in plain battle seems to me by no means one of the most terrible things in this very terrible world. Of course, one of them (at least) must be mistaken. And of course war is a very great evil. But that is not the question. The question is whether war is the greatest evil in the world, so that any state of affairs which might result from submission is certainly preferable. And I do not see any really cogent arguments for that view.

Another attempt to get a Pacifist conclusion

from the intuition is of a more political and calculating kind. If not the greatest evil, yet war is a great evil. Therefore, we should all like to remove it if we can. But every war leads to another war. The removal of war must therefore be attempted. We must increase by propaganda the number of Pacifists in each nation until it becomes great enough to deter that nation from going to war. This seem to me wild work. Only liberal societies tolerate Pacifists. In the liberal society, the number of Pacifists will either be large enough to cripple the state as a belligerent, or not. If not, you have done nothing. If it is large enough, then you have handed over the state which does tolerate Pacifists to its totalitarian neighbour who does not. Pacifism of this kind is taking the straight road to a world in which there will be no Pacifists.

It may be asked whether, faint as the hope is of abolishing war by Pacifism, there is any other hope. But the question belongs to a mode of thought which I find quite alien to me. It consists in assuming that the great permanent miseries in human life must be curable if only we can find the right cure; and it then proceeds by elimination and concludes that whatever is left, however unlikely to prove a cure, must nevertheless do so. Hence the fanaticism of Marxists, Freudians, Eugenists, Spiritualists, Douglasites, Federal Unionists, Vegetarians, and all the rest. But I have received no assurance that anything we can do will eradicate suffering. I think the best results are obtained by people who work quietly away at limited objectives, such as the abolition of the slave trade, or prison reform, or factory acts, or tuberculosis, not by those who think they can achieve universal justice, or health, or peace. I think the art of life consists in tackling each immediate evil as well as we can. To avert or postpone one particular war by wise policy, or to render one particular campaign shorter by strength and skill or less terrible by mercy to the conquered and the civilians is more useful than all the proposals for universal peace that have ever been made; just as the dentist who can stop one toothache has deserved better of humanity than all the men who think they have some scheme for producing a perfectly healthy race.

I do not therefore find any very clear and cogent reason for inferring from the general principle of beneficence the conclusion that I must disobey if I am called on by lawful authority to be a soldier. I turn next to consider Authority. Authority is either special or general, and again either human or divine.

The special human authority which rests on me in this matter is that of the society to which I belong. That society by its declaration of war has decided the issue against Pacifism in this particular instance, and by its institutions and practice for centuries has decided against Pacifism in general. If I am a Pacifist, I have Arthur and Aelfred, Elizabeth and Cromwell, Walpole and Burke, against me. I have my university, my school, and my parents against me. I have the literature of my country against me, and cannot even open my *Beowulf*, my Shakespeare, my Johnson, or my Wordsworth without being reproved. Now, of course, this authority of England is not final. But there is a difference between conclusive authority and authority of no weight at all. Men may differ as to the weight they would give the almost unanimous authority of England. I am not here concerned with assessing it but merely with noting that whatever weight it has is against Pacifism. And, of course, my duty to take that authority into account is increased by the fact that I am indebted to that society for my birth and my upbringing, for the education which has allowed me to become a Pacifist, and the tolerant laws which allow me to remain one.

So much for special human authority. The sentence of general human authority is equally clear. From the dawn of history down to the sinking of the *Terris Bay*, the world echoes with the praise of righteous war. To be a Pacifist, I must part company with Homer and Virgil, with Plato and Aristotle, with Zarathustra and the *Bhagavad-Gita*, with Cicero and Montaigne, with Iceland and with Egypt. From this point of view, I am almost tempted to reply to the Pacifist as Johnson replied to Goldsmith, "Nay Sir, if you will not take the universal opinion of mankind, I have no more to say."

I am aware that, though Hooker thought "the general and perpetual voice of men is as the sentence of God Himself," yet many who hear will give it little or no weight. This disregard of human authority may have two roots. It may spring from the belief that human history is a simple, unilinear movement from worse to better—what is called a belief in Progress—so that any given generation is always in all respects wiser than all previous generations. To those who believe thus, our ancestors are superseded and there seems nothing improbable in the claim that the whole world was wrong until the day before yesterday and now has suddenly become right. With such people I confess I cannot argue, for I do not share their basic assumption.

Believers in progress rightly note that in the world of machines the new model supersedes the old; from this they falsely infer a similar kind of supercession in such things as virtue and wisdom.

But human authority may be discounted on a quite different ground. It may be held, at least by a Christian Pacifist, that the human race is fallen and corrupt, so that even the consent of great and wise human teachers and great nations widely separated in time and place affords no clue whatsoever to the good. If this contention is being made, we must then turn to our next head, that of Divine Authority.

I shall consider Divine Authority only in terms of Christianity. Of the other civilised religions I believe that only one—Buddhism—is genuinely Pacifist; and anyway I am not well enough informed about them to discuss them with profit. And when we turn to Christianity, we find Pacifism based almost exclusively on certain of the sayings of Our Lord Himself. If those sayings do not establish the Pacifist position, it is vain to try to base it on the general *securus judicat* of Christendom as a whole. For when I seek guidance there, I find Authority on the whole against me. Looking at the statement which is my immediate authority as an Anglican, the Thirty-Nine Articles, I find it laid down in black and white that "it is lawful for Christian men, at the commandment of the Magistrate, to wear weapons and serve in the wars." Dissenters may not accept this; then I can refer them to the history of the Presbyterians, which is by no means Pacifist. Papists may not accept this; then I can refer them to the ruling of Thomas Aquinas that "even as princes lawfully defend their land by the sword against disturbance from within, so it belongs to them to defend it by the sword from enemies without." Or if you demand patristic authority, I give you St. Augustine, "If Christian discipleship wholly reprobated war, then to those who sought the counsel of salvation in the Gospel this answer would have been given first, that they should throw away their arms and withdraw themselves altogether from being soldiers. But what was really said to them was, 'Do violence to no man and be content with your pay.' When he bade them to be content with their due soldiers' pay, he forbade them not to be paid as soldiers." But of checking individual voices, there would be no end. All bodies that claim to be Churches—that is, who claim apostolic succession and accept the Creeds—have constantly blessed what they regarded as righteous arms. Doctors, bishops, and popes—including, I think, the present Pope [Pius XII]—have again and again discountenanced the Pacifist position. Nor, I think, do we find a word about Pacifism in the apostolic writings, which are older than the Gospels and represent, if anything does, that original Christendom whereof the Gospels themselves are a product.

The whole Christian case for Pacifism rests, therefore, on certain Dominical utterances, such as "Resist not evil: but whosoever shall smite thee on thy right cheek, turn to him the other also." I am now to deal with the Christian who says this is to be taken without qualification. I need not point out —for it has doubtless been pointed out to you before—that such a Christian is obliged to take all the other hard sayings of Our Lord in the same way. For the man who has done so, who has on every occasion given to all who ask him and has finally

given all he has to the poor, no one will fail to feel
respect. With such a man I must suppose myself to
be arguing; for who would deem worth answering
that inconsistent person who takes Our Lord's
words *à la rigueur* when they dispense him from a
possible obligation and takes them with latitude
when they demand that he should become a pauper?

There are three ways of taking the command to
turn the other cheek. One is the Pacifist interpretation; it means what it says and imposes a duty of
nonresistance on all men in all circumstances. Another is the minimising interpretation; it does not
mean what it says but is merely an orientally hyper-
bolical way of saying that you should put up with
a lot and be placable. Both you and I agree in re-
jecting this view. The conflict is therefore between
the Pacifist interpretation and a third one which
I am now going to propound. I think the text means
exactly what it says, but with an understood reservation in favour of those obviously exceptional
cases which every hearer would naturally assume to
be exceptions without being told. Or to put the
same thing in more logical language, I think the
duty of nonresistance is here stated as regards
injuries *simpliciter*, but without prejudice to anything we may have to allow later about injuries
secundum quid. That is, insofar as the only relevant
factors in the case are an injury to me by my neighbour and a desire on my part to retaliate, then I
hold that Christianity commands the absolute mortification of that desire. No quarter whatever is
given to the voice within us which says, "He's done
it to me, so I'll do the same to him." But the moment you introduce other factors, of course, the
problem is altered. Does anyone suppose that Our

Lord's hearers understood Him to mean that if a
homicidal maniac, attempting to murder a third
party, tried to knock me out of the way, I must
stand aside and let him get his victim? I at any rate
think it impossible they could have so understood
Him. I think it equally impossible that they supposed Him to mean that the best way of bringing
up a child was to let it hit its parents whenever it
was in a temper, or, when it had grabbed at the
jam, to give it the honey also. I think the meaning
of the words was perfectly clear—"Insofar as you
are simply an angry man who has been hurt, mortify
your anger and do not hit back"—even, one would
have assumed that insofar as you are a magistrate
struck by a private person, a parent struck by a
child, a teacher by a scholar, a sane man by a lunatic, or a soldier by the public enemy, your duties
may be very different, different because they may
be then other motives than egoistic retaliation for
hitting back. Indeed, as the audience were private
people in a disarmed nation, it seems unlikely that
they would have ever supposed Our Lord to be
referring to war. War was not what they would have
been thinking of. The frictions of daily life among
villagers were more likely to be in their minds.

That is my chief reason for preferring this interpretation to yours. Any saying is to be taken in the
sense it would naturally have borne in the time
and place of utterance. But I also think that, so
taken, it harmonises better with St. John Baptist's
words to the soldiers and with the fact that one of
the few persons whom Our Lord praised without
reservation was a Roman centurion. It also allows
me to suppose that the New Testament is consistent
with itself. St. Paul approves of the magistrate's

use of the sword (Romans 13:4) and so does St.
Peter (I Peter 2:14). If Our Lord's words are taken
in the unqualified sense which the Pacifist demands,
we shall then be forced to the conclusion that
Christ's true meaning, concealed from those who
lived in the same time and spoke the same language, and whom He Himself chose to be His
messengers to the world, as well as from all their
successors, has at last been discovered in our own
time. I know there are people who will not find
this sort of thing difficult to believe, just as there
are people ready to maintain that the true meaning
of Plato or Shakespeare, oddly concealed from their
contemporaries and immediate successors, has pre-
served its virginity for the daring embraces of one
or two modern professors. But I cannot apply to
divine matters a method of exegesis which I have
already rejected with contempt in my profane
studies. Any theory which bases itself on a supposed "historical Jesus" to be dug out of the Gospels and then set up in opposition to Christian
teaching is suspect. There have been too many historical Jesuses—a liberal Jesus, a pneumatic Jesus,
a Barthian Jesus, a Marxist Jesus. They are the
cheap crop of each publisher's list, like the new
Napoleons and new Queen Victorias. It is not to
such phantoms that I look for my faith and my
salvation.

Christian authority, then, fails me in my search
for Pacifism. It remains to inquire whether, if I
still remain a Pacifist, I ought to suspect the secret
influence of any passion. I hope you will not here
misunderstand me. I do not intend to join in any
of the jibes to which those of your persuasion are
exposed in the popular press. Let me say at the

outset that I think it unlikely there is anyone present less courageous than myself. But let me also say that there is no man alive so virtuous that he need feel himself insulted at being asked to consider the possibility of a warping passion when the choice is one between so much happiness and so much misery. For let us make no mistake. All that we fear from all the kinds of adversity, severally, is collected together in the life of a soldier on active service. Like sickness, it threatens pain and death. Like poverty, it threatens ill lodging, cold, heat, thirst, and hunger. Like slavery, it threatens toil, humiliation, injustice, and arbitrary rule. Like exile, it separates you from all you love. Like the gallies, it imprisons you at close quarters with uncongenial companions. It threatens *every* temporal evil—every evil except dishonour and final perdition, and those who bear it like it no better than you would like it. On the other side, though it may not be your fault, it is certainly a fact that Pacifism threatens you with almost nothing. Some public opprobrium, yes, from people whose opinion you discount and whose society you do not frequent, soon recompensed by the warm mutual approval which exists, inevitably, in any minority group. For the rest it offers you a continuance of the life you know and love, among the people and in the surroundings you know and love. It offers you time to lay the foundations of a career; for whether you will or no, you can hardly help getting the jobs for which the discharged soldiers will one day look in vain. You do not even have to fear, as Pacifists may have had to fear in the last war, that public opinion will punish you when the peace comes. For we have learned now that though the world is slow to forgive, it is quick to forget.

This, then, is why I am not a Pacifist. If I tried to become one, I should find a very doubtful factual basis, an obscure train of reasoning, a weight of authority both human and Divine against me, and strong grounds for suspecting that my wishes had directed my decision. As I have said, moral decisions do not admit of mathematical certainty. It may be, after all, that Pacifism is right. But it seems to me very long odds, longer odds than I would care to take with the voice of almost all humanity against me.

TRANSPOSITION

In the church to which I belong this day is set apart for commemorating the descent of the Holy Ghost upon the first Christians shortly after the Ascension. I want to consider one of the phenomena which accompanied, or followed, this descent: the phenomenon which our translation calls "speaking with tongues" and which the learned call *glossolalia*. You will not suppose that I think this the most important aspect of Pentecost, but I have two reasons for selecting it. In the first place it would be ridiculous for me to speak about the nature of the Holy Ghost or the modes of His operation; that would be an attempt to teach when I have nearly all to learn. In the second place, *glossolalia* has often been a stumbling block to me. It is, to be frank, an embarrassing phenomenon. St. Paul himself seems to have been rather embarrassed by it in 1 Corinthians and labours to turn the desire and the attention of the Church to more obviously edifying gifts. But he goes no further. He throws in almost parenthetically the statement that he himself spoke with tongues more than anyone else, and he does not question the spiritual, or supernatural, source of the phenomenon.

The difficulty I feel is this. On the one hand, *glossolalia* has remained an intermittent "variety of religious experience" down to the present day. Every now and then we hear that in some revivalist meeting one or more of those present has burst into a torrent of what appears to be gibberish. The thing does not seem to be edifying, and all non-Christian opinion would regard it as a kind of hysteria, an involuntary discharge of nervous excitement. A good deal even of Christian opinion would explain most instances of it in exactly the same way; and I must confess that it would be very hard to believe that in all instances of it the Holy Ghost is operating. We suspect, even if we cannot be sure, that it is usually an affair of the nerves. That is one horn of the dilemma. On the other hand, we cannot as Christians shelve the story of Pentecost or deny that there, at any rate, the speaking with tongues was miraculous. For the men spoke not gibberish but languages unknown to them, though known to other people present. And the whole event of which this makes part is built into the very fabric of the birth story of the Church. It is this very event which the risen Lord had told the Church to wait for—almost in the last words He uttered before His ascension. It looks, therefore, as if we shall have to say that the very same phenomenon which is sometimes not only natural but even pathological is at other times (or at least at one other time) the organ of the Holy Ghost. And this seems at first very surprising and very open to attack. The sceptic will certainly seize this opportunity to talk to us about Occam's razor, to accuse us of multiplying hypotheses. If most instances of *glossolalia* are covered by hysteria, is it not (he will ask) extremely probable that that explanation covers the remaining instances too?

It is to this difficulty that I would gladly bring a little ease if I can. And I will begin by pointing out that it belongs to a class of difficulties. The closest parallel to it within that class is raised by the erotic language and imagery we find in the mystics. In them we find a whole range of expressions—and therefore possibly of emotions—with which we are quite familiar in another context and which, in that other context, have a clear, natural significance. But in the mystical writings it is claimed that these elements have a different cause. And once more the sceptic will ask why the cause which we are content to accept for ninety-nine instances of such language should not be held to cover the hundredth too. The hypothesis that mysticism is an erotic phenomenon will seem to him immensely more probable than any other.

Put in its most general terms, our problem is that of the obvious continuity between things which are admittedly natural and things which, it is claimed, are spiritual; the reappearance in what professes to be our supernatural life of all the same old elements which make up our natural life and (it would seem) of no others. If we have really been visited by a revelation from beyond Nature, is it not very strange that an Apocalypse can furnish heaven with nothing more than selections from terrestrial experience (crowns, thrones, and music), that devotion can find no language but that of human lovers, and that the rite whereby Christians enact a mystical union should turn out to be only the old, familiar act of of eating and drinking? And you may add that the very same problem also breaks out on a lower level, not only between spiritual and natural but also between higher and lower levels of the natural life. Hence cynics very plausibly challenge our civilised conception of the difference between love and lust by pointing out that when all is said and done they usually end in what is, physically, the same act. They similarly challenge the difference between justice and revenge on the ground that what finally happens to the criminal may be the same. And in all these cases, let us admit that the cynics and sceptics have a good *prima facie* case. The same acts do reappear in justice as well as in revenge; the consummation of humanised and conjugal love is physiologically the same as that of the merely biological lust; religious language and imagery, and probably religious emotion too, contains nothing that has not been borrowed from Nature.

Now it seems to me that the only way to refute the critic here is to show that the same *prima facie* case is equally plausible in some instance where we all know (not by faith or by logic, but empirically) that it is in fact false. Can we find an instance of higher and lower where the higher is within almost everyone's experience? I think we can. Consider the following quotation from *Pepys's Diary*:

With my wife to the King's House to see *The Virgin Martyr*, and it is mighty pleasant. . . . But that which did please me beyond anything in the whole world was the wind musick when the angel comes down, which is so sweet that it ravished me and, indeed, in a word, did wrap up my soul so that it made me really sick, just as I have formerly been when in love with my wife . . . and makes me resolve to practise wind musick and to make my wife do the like. (27 February 1668.)

There are several points here that deserve attention: (1) that the internal sensation accompanying intense aesthetic delight was indistinguishable from the sensation accompanying two other experiences, that of being in love and that of being, say, in a rough channel crossing; (2) that of these two other experiences, one at least is the very reverse of pleasurable; no man enjoys nausea; (3) that Pepys was, nevertheless, anxious to have again the experience whose sensational accompaniment was identical with the very unpleasant accompaniments of sickness; that was why he decided to take up wind music.

Now it may be true that not many of us have fully shared Pepys's experience, but we have all experienced that sort of thing. For myself I find that if, during a moment of intense aesthetic rapture, one tries to turn round and catch by introspection what one is actually feeling, one can never lay one's hand on anything but a physical sensation. In my case it is a kind of kick or flutter in the diaphragm. Perhaps that is all Pepys meant by "really sick." But the important point is this: I find that this kick or flutter is exactly the same sensation which, in me, accompanies great and sudden anguish. Introspection can discover no difference at all between my neural response to very bad news and my neural response to the overture of *The Magic Flute*. If I were to judge simply by sensations, I should come to the absurd conclusion that joy and anguish are the same thing, that what I most dread is the same with what I most desire. Introspection discovers nothing more or different in the one than in the other. And I expect that most of you, if you are in the habit of noticing such things, will report more or less the same.

Now let us take a step farther. These sensations —Pepys's sickness and my flutter in the diaphragm —do not merely accompany very different experi-

ences as an irrelevant or neutral addition. We may
be quite sure that Pepys hated that sensation when
it came in real sickness, and we know from his own
words that he liked it when it came with wind
music, for he took measures to make as sure as possible of getting it again. And I likewise love this
internal flutter in one context and call it a pleasure
and hate it in another and call it misery. It is not a
mere sign of joy and anguish; it becomes what it
signifies. When the joy thus flows over into the
nerves, that overflow is its consummation; when
the anguish thus flows over, that physical symptom
is the crowning horror. The very same thing which
makes the sweetest drop of all in the sweet cup also
makes the bitterest drop in the bitter.

And here, I suggest, we have found what we are
looking for. I take our emotional life to be "higher"
than the life of our sensations—not, of course,
morally higher, but richer, more varied, more subtle.
And this is a higher level which nearly all of us
know. And I believe that if anyone watches carefully the relation between his emotions and his
sensations he will discover the following facts: (1)
that the nerves do respond, and in a sense most
adequately and exquisitely, to the emotions; (2)
that their resources are far more limited, the possible variations of sense far fewer, than those of
emotion; and (3) that the senses compensate for this
by using the *same* sensation to express more than
one emotion—even, as we have seen, to express
opposite emotions.

Where we tend to go wrong is in assuming that
if there is to be a correspondence between two systems it must be a one-for-one correspondence—that
A in the one system must be represented by *a* in the

other, and so on. But the correspondence between emotion and sensation turns out not to be of that sort. And there never could be correspondence of that sort where the one system was really richer than the other. If the richer system is to be represented in the poorer at all, this can only be by giving each element in the poorer system more than one meaning. The transposition of the richer into the poorer must, so to speak, be algebraical, not arithmetical. If you are to translate from a language which has a large vocabulary into a language that has a small vocabulary, then you must be allowed to use several words in more than one sense. If you are to write a language with twenty-two vowel sounds in an alphabet with only five vowel characters, then you must be allowed to give each of those five characters more than one value. If you are making a piano version of a piece originally scored for an orchestra, then the same piano notes which represent flutes in one passage must also represent violins in another.

As the examples show, we are all quite familiar with this kind of transposition or adaptation from a richer to a poorer medium. The most familiar example of all is the art of drawing. The problem here is to represent a three-dimensional world on a flat sheet of paper. The solution is perspective, and perspective means that we must give more than one value to a two-dimensional shape. Thus in a drawing of a cube, we use an acute angle to represent what is a right angle in the real world. But elsewhere an acute angle on the paper may represent what was already an acute angle in the real world, for example, the point of a spear or the gable of a house. The very same shape which you must draw to give the illusion of a straight road receding from the spectator is also the shape you draw for a dunce's cap. As with the lines, so with the shading. Your brightest light in the picture is, in literal fact, only plain white paper, and this must do for the sun, or a lake in evening light, or snow, or human flesh.

I now make two comments on the instances of Transposition which are already before us:

1. It is clear that in each case what is happening in the lower medium can be understood only if we know the higher medium. The instance where this knowledge is most commonly lacking is the musical one. The piano version means one thing to the musician who knows the original orchestral score and another thing to the man who hears it simply as a piano piece. But the second man would be at an even greater disadvantage if he had never heard any instrument but a piano and even doubted the existence of other instruments. Even more, we understand pictures only because we know and inhabit the three-dimensional world. If we can imagine a creature who perceived only two dimensions and yet could somehow be aware of the lines as he crawled over them on the paper, we shall easily see how impossible it would be for him to understand. At first he might be prepared to accept on authority our assurance that there was a world in three dimensions. But when we pointed to the lines on the paper and tried to explain, say, that "this is a road," would he not reply that the shape which we were asking him to accept as a revelation of our mysterious other world was the very same shape which, on our own showing, elsewhere meant nothing but a triangle. And soon, I think, he would say, "You

keep on telling me of this other world and its unimaginable shapes which you call solid. But isn't it very suspicious that all the shapes which you offer me as images or reflections of the solid ones turn out on inspection to be simply the old two-dimensional shapes of my own world as I have always known it? Is it not obvious that your vaunted other world, so far from being the archetype, is a dream which borrows all its elements from this one?"

2. It is of some importance to notice that the word *symbolism* is not adequate in all cases to cover the relation between the higher medium and its transposition in the lower. It covers some cases perfectly, but not others. Thus the relation between speech and writing is one of symbolism. The written characters exist solely for the eye, the spoken words solely for the ear. There is complete discontinuity between them. They are not like one another, nor does the one cause the other to be. The one is simply a *sign* of the other and signifies it by a convention. But a picture is not related to the visible world in just that way. Pictures are part of the visible world themselves and represent it only by being part of it. Their visibility has the same source. The suns and lamps in pictures seem to shine only because real suns or lamps shine on them; that is, they seem to shine a great deal because they really shine a little in reflecting their archetypes. The sunlight in a picture is therefore not related to real sunlight simply as written words are to spoken. It is a sign, but also something more than a sign, and only a sign because it is also more than a sign, because in it the thing signified is really in a certain mode present. If I had to name the relation I should call

it not symbolical but sacramental. But in the case we started from—that of emotion and sensation—we are even further beyond mere symbolism. For there, as we have seen, the very same sensation does not merely accompany, nor merely signify, diverse and opposite emotions, but becomes part of them. The emotion descends bodily, as it were, into the sensation and digests, transforms, transubstantiates it, so that the same thrill along the nerves *is* delight or *is* agony.

I am not going to maintain that what I call Transposition is the only possible mode whereby a poorer medium can respond to a richer, but I claim that it is very hard to imagine any other. It is therefore, at the very least, not improbable that Transposition occurs whenever the higher reproduces itself in the lower. Thus, to digress for a moment, it seems to me very likely that the real relation between mind and body is one of Transposition. We are certain that, in this life at any rate, thought is intimately connected with the brain. The theory that thought therefore is merely a movement in the brain is, in my opinion, nonsense, for if so, that theory itself would be merely a movement, an event among atoms, which may have speed and direction, but of which it would be meaningless to use the words "true" or "false." We are driven then to some kind of correspondence. But if we assume a one-for-one correspondence, this means that we have to attribute an almost unbelievable complexity and variety of events to the brain. But I submit that a one-for-one relation is probably quite unnecessary. All our examples suggest that the brain can respond—in a sense, adequately and exquisitely correspond—to the seem-

ingly infinite variety of consciousness without providing one single physical modification for each
single modification of consciousness.

But that is a digression. Let us now return to
our original question about Spirit and Nature,
God and Man. Our problem was that in what
claims to be our spiritual life all the elements of our
natural life recur, and, what is worse, it looks at
first glance as if no other elements were present.
We now see that if the spiritual is richer than the
natural (as no one who believes in its existence
would deny), then this is exactly what we should
expect. And the sceptic's conclusion that the so-
called spiritual is really derived from the natural,
that it is a mirage or projection or imaginary ex-
tension of the natural, is also exactly what we should
expect, for, as we have seen, this is the mistake that
an observer who knew only the lower medium
would be bound to make in every case of Transposition. The brutal man never can by analysis
find anything but lust in love; the Flatlander never
can find anything but flat shapes in a picture;
physiology never can find anything in thought except twitchings of the grey matter. It is no good
browbeating the critic who approaches a Transposition from below. On the evidence available to
him his conclusion is the only one possible.

Everything is different when you approach the
Transposition from above, as we all do in the case
of emotion and sensation or of the three-dimensional
world and pictures, and as the spiritual man does
in the case we are considering. Those who spoke
with tongues, as St. Paul did, can well understand
how that holy phenomenon differed from the hys-
terical phenomen—although be it remembered,

they were in a sense exactly the same phenomenon, just as the very same sensation came to Pepys in love, in the enjoyment of music, and in sickness. Spiritual things are spiritually discerned. The spiritual man judges all things and is judged of none.

But who dares to be a spiritual man? In the full sense, none of us. And yet we are somehow aware that we approach from above, or from inside, at least some of those Transpositions which embody the Christian life in this world. With whatever sense of unworthiness, with whatever sense of audacity, we must affirm that we know a little of the higher system which is being transposed. In a way the claim we are making is not a very startling one. We are only claiming to know that our apparent devotion, whatever else it may have been, was not simply erotic, or that our apparent desire for Heaven, whatever else it may have been, was not simply a desire for longevity or jewellery or social splendours. Perhaps we have never really attained at all to what St. Paul would describe as spiritual life. But at the very least we know, in some dim and confused way, that we were trying to use natural acts and images and language with a new value, have at least desired a repentance which was not merely prudential and a love which was not self-centred. At the worst, we know enough of the spiritual to know that we have fallen short of it, as if the picture knew enough of the three-dimensional world to be aware that it was flat.

It is not only for humility's sake (that, of course) that we must emphasise the dimness of our knowledge. I suspect that, save by God's direct miracle, spiritual experience can never abide introspection. If even our emotions will not do so (since the attempt to find out what we are now *feeling* yields nothing more than a physical sensation), much less will the operations of the Holy Ghost. The attempt to discover by introspective analysis our own spiritual condition is to me a horrible thing which reveals, at best, not the secrets of God's spirit and ours, but their transpositions in intellect, emotion, and imagination, and which at worst may be the quickest road to presumption or despair.

I believe that this doctrine of Transposition provides for most of us a background very much needed for the theological virtue of Hope. We can hope only for what we can desire. And the trouble is that any adult and philosophically respectable notion we can form of Heaven is forced to deny of that state most of the things our nature desires. There is no doubt a blessedly ingenuous faith, a child's or a savage's faith which finds no difficulty. It accepts without awkward questionings the harps and golden streets and the family reunions pictured by hymn writers. Such a faith is deceived, yet, in the deepest sense, not deceived, for while it errs in mistaking symbol for fact, yet it apprehends Heaven as joy and plenitude and love. But it is impossible for most of us. And we must not try, by artifice, to make ourselves more naïf than we are. A man does not "become as a little child" by aping childhood. Hence our notion of Heaven involves perpetual negations: no food, no drink, no sex, no movement, no mirth, no events, no time, no art.

Against all these, to be sure, we set one positive: the vision and enjoyment of God. And since this is an infinite good, we hold (rightly) that it outweighs them all. That is, the reality of the Beatific Vision would or will outweigh, would infinitely outweigh, the reality of the negations. But can our present notion of it outweigh our present notion of them? That is quite a different question. And for most of us at most times the answer is no. How it may be for great saints and mystics I cannot tell. But for others the conception of that Vision is a difficult, precarious, and fugitive extrapolation from a very few and ambiguous moments in our earthly experience, while our idea of the negated natural goods is vivid and persistent, loaded with the memories of a lifetime, built into our nerves and muscles and therefore into our imaginations.

Thus the negatives have, so to speak, an unfair advantage in every competition with the positive. What is worse, their presence—and most when we most resolutely try to suppress or ignore them— vitiates even such a faint and ghostlike notion of the positive as we might have had. The exclusion of the lower goods begins to seem the essential characteristic of the higher good. We feel, if we do not say, that the vision of God will come not to fulfil but to destroy our nature; this bleak fantasy often underlies our very use of such words as "holy" or "pure" or "spiritual."

We must not allow this to happen if we can possibly prevent it. We must believe—and therefore in some degree imagine—that every negation will be only the reverse side of a fulfilling. And we must mean by that the fulfilling, precisely, of our humanity, not our transformation into angels nor our absorption into Deity. For though we shall be "as the angels" and made "like unto" our Master, I think this means "like with the likeness proper to men" as different instruments that play the same air but each in its own fashion. How far the life of the risen man will be sensory, we do not know. But I surmise that it will differ from the sensory life we know here, not as emptiness differs from water or water from wine but as a flower differs from a bulb or a cathedral from an architect's drawing. And it is here that Transposition helps me.

Let us construct a fable. Let us picture a woman thrown into a dungeon. There she bears and rears a son. He grows up seeing nothing but the dungeon walls, the straw on the floor, and a little patch of the sky seen through the grating, which is too high up to show anything except sky. This unfortunate woman was an artist, and when they imprisoned her she managed to bring with her a drawing pad and a box of pencils. As she never loses the hope of deliverance, she is constantly teaching her son about that outer world which he has never seen. She does it very largely by drawing him pictures. With her pencil she attempts to show him what fields, rivers, mountains, cities, and waves on a beach are like. He is a dutiful boy and he does his best to believe her when she tells him that that outer world is far more interesting and glorious than anything in the dungeon. At times he succeeds. On the whole he gets on tolerably well until, one day, he says something that gives his mother pause. For a minute or two they are at cross-purposes. Finally it dawns on her that he has, all these years, lived under a misconception. "But," she gasps, "you didn't think that the real world was full of lines drawn in lead pencil?" "What?" says the boy. "No pencil marks there?" And instantly his whole notion of the outer world becomes a blank. For the lines, by which alone he was imagining it, have now been denied of it. He has no idea of that which will exclude and dispense with the lines, that of which the lines were merely a transposition—the waving treetops, the light dancing on the weir, the coloured three-dimensional realities which are not enclosed in lines but define their own shapes at every moment with a delicacy and multiplicity which no drawing could ever achieve. The child will get the idea that the real world is somehow less visible than his mother's pictures. In reality it lacks lines because it is incomparably more visible.

So with us. "We know not what we shall be"; but we may be sure we shall be more, not less, than we were on earth. Our natural experiences (sensory, emotional, imaginative) are only like the drawing, like pencilled lines on flat paper. If they vanish in the risen life, they will vanish only as pencil lines vanish from the real landscape, not as a candle flame that is put out but as a candle flame which becomes invisible because someone has pulled up the blind, thrown open the shutters, and let in the blaze of the risen sun.

You can put it whichever way you please. You can say that by Transposition our humanity, senses and all, can be made the vehicle of beatitude. Or you can say that the heavenly bounties by Transposition are embodied during this life in our temporal experience. But the second way is the better. It is the present life which is the diminution, the symbol, the etiolated, the (as it were) "vegetarian" substitute. If flesh and blood cannot inherit the Kingdom, that is not because they are too solid, too gross, too distinct, too "illustrious with being." They are too flimsy, too transitory, too phantasmal.

With this, my case, as the lawyers say, is complete. But I have just four points to add:

1. I hope it is quite clear that the conception of Transposition, as I call it, is distinct from another conception often used for the same purpose—I mean the conception of development. The Developmentalist explains the continuity between things that claim to be spiritual and things that are certainly natural by saying that the one slowly turned into the other. I believe this view explains some facts, but I think it has been much overworked. At any rate it is not the theory I am putting forward. I am not saying that the natural act of eating after millions of years somehow blossoms into the Christian sacrament. I am saying that the Spiritual Reality, which existed before there were any creatures who ate, gives this natural act a new meaning, and more than a new meaning: makes it in a certain context to be a different thing. In a word, I think that real landscapes enter into pictures, not that pictures will one day sprout out into real trees and grass.

2. I have found it impossible, in thinking of what I call Transposition, not to ask myself whether it may help us to conceive the Incarnation. Of course if Transposition were merely a mode of symbolism it could give us no help at all in this matter; on the contrary, it would lead us wholly astray, back into a new kind of Docetism (or would it be only the old kind?) and away from the utterly historical and concrete reality which is the centre of all our hope, faith, and love. But then, as I have pointed out, Transposition is not always symbolism. In varying degrees the lower reality can actually be drawn into the higher and become part of it. The sensation which accompanies joy becomes itself joy; we can hardly choose but say "incarnates joy." If this is so,

then I venture to suggest, though with great doubt and in the most provisional way, that the concept of Transposition may have some contribution to make to the theology—or at least to the philosophy —of the Incarnation. For we are told in one of the creeds that the Incarnation worked "not by conversion of the Godhead into flesh, but by taking of the Manhood into God." And it seems to me that there is a real analogy between this and what I have called Transposition: that humanity, still remaining itself, is not merely counted as, but veritably drawn into, Deity, seems to me like what happens when a sensation (not in itself a pleasure) is drawn into the joy it accompanies. But I walk *in mirabilibus supra me* and submit all to the verdict of real theologians.

3. I have tried to stress throughout the inevitableness of the error made about every transposition by one who approaches it from the lower medium only. The strength of such a critic lies in the words "merely" or "nothing but." He sees all the facts but not the meaning. Quite truly, therefore, he claims to have seen all the facts. There *is* nothing else there; except the meaning. He is therefore, as regards the matter in hand, in the position of an animal. You will have noticed that most dogs cannot understand *pointing*. You point to a bit of food on the floor; the dog, instead of looking at the floor, sniffs at your finger. A finger is a finger to him, and that is all. His world is all fact and no meaning. And in a period when factual realism is dominant we shall find people deliberately inducing upon themselves this doglike mind. A man who has experienced love from within will deliberately go about to inspect it analytically from outside and

regard the results of this analysis as truer than his experience. The extreme limit of this self-binding is seen in those who, like the rest of us, have consciousness, yet go about to study the human organism as if they did not know it was conscious. As long as this deliberate refusal to understand things from above, even where such understanding is possible, continues, it is idle to talk of any final victory over materialism. The critique of every experience from below, the voluntary ignoring of meaning and concentration on fact, will always have the same plausibility. There will always be evidence, and every month fresh evidence, to show that religion is only psychological, justice only self-protection, politics only economics, love only lust, and thought itself only cerebral biochemistry.

4. Finally, I suggest that what has been said of Transposition throws a new light on the doctrine of the resurrection of the body. For in a sense Transposition can do anything. However great the difference between Spirit and Nature, between aesthetic joy and that flutter in the diaphragm, between reality and picture, yet the Transposition can be in its own way adequate. I said before that in your drawing you had only plain white paper for sun and cloud, snow, water, and human flesh. In one sense, how miserably inadequate! Yet in another, how perfect. If the shadows are properly done, that patch of white paper will, in some curious way, be very like blazing sunshine; we shall almost feel cold while we look at the paper snow and almost warm our hands at the paper fire. May we not, by a reasonable analogy, suppose likewise that there is no experience of the spirit so transcendent and supernatural, no vision of Diety Himself so close and

so far beyond all images and emotions, that to it also there cannot be an appropriate correspondence on the sensory level? Not by a new sense but by the incredible flooding of those very sensations we now have with a meaning, a transvaluation, of which we have here no faintest guess?

IS THEOLOGY
POETRY?

The question I have been asked to discuss tonight
—"Is Theology Poetry?"—is not of my own choos-
ing. I find myself, in fact, in the position of a
candidate at an examination, and I must obey the
advice of my tutors by first making sure that I know
what the question means.

By *Theology* we mean, I suppose, the systematic
series of statements about God and about man's relation to Him which the believers of a religion
make. And in a paper sent me by this Club I may
perhaps assume that Theology means principally
Christian Theology. I am the bolder to make this
assumption because something of what I think about
other religions will appear in what I have to say.
It must also be remembered that only a minority
of the religions of the world have a theology. There
was no systematic series of statements which the
Greeks agreed in believing about Zeus.

The other term, *Poetry*, is much harder to define,
but I believe I can assume the question which my
examiners had in mind without a definition. There
are certain things which I feel sure they were not
asking me. They were not asking me whether Theology is written in verse. They were not asking me
whether most theologians are masters of a "simple,
sensuous, and passionate" style. I believe they
meant, "Is Theology *merely* poetry?" This might
be expanded: "Does Theology offer us, at best, only

that kind of truth which, according to some critics, poetry offers us?" And the first difficulty of answering the question in that form is that we have no general agreement as to what "poetical truth" means, or whether there is really any such thing. It will be best, therefore, to use for this paper a very vague and modest notion of poetry, simply as writing which arouses and in part satisfies the imagination. And I shall take it that the question I am to answer is this: Does Christian Theology owe its attraction to its power of arousing and satisfying our imaginations? Are those who believe it mistaking aesthetic enjoyment for intellectual assent, or assenting because they enjoy?

Faced with this question, I naturally turn to inspect the believer whom I know best—myself. And the first fact I discover, or seem to discover, is that for me at any rate, if Theology is Poetry, it is not very good poetry.

Considered as poetry, the doctrine of the Trinity seems to me to fall between two stools. It has neither the monolithic grandeur of strictly Unitarian conceptions nor the richness of Polytheism. The omnipotence of God is not, to my taste, a poetical advantage. Odin, fighting against enemies who are not his own creatures and who will in fact defeat him in the end, has a heroic appeal which the God of Christians cannot have. There is also a certain bareness about the Christian picture of the universe. A future state and orders of superhuman creatures are held to exist, but only the slightest hints of their nature are offered. Finally, and worst of all, the whole cosmic story, though full of tragic elements, yet fails of being a tragedy. Christianity offers the attractions neither of optimism nor of pessimism. It represents the life of the universe as being very like the mortal life of men on this planet—"of a mingled yarn, good and ill together." The majestic simplifications of Pantheism and the tangled wood of Pagan animism both seem to me, in their different ways, more attractive. Christianity just misses the tidiness of the one and the delicious variety of the other. For I take it there are two things the imagination loves to do. It loves to embrace its object completely, to take it in at a single glance, and see it as something harmonious, symmetrical, and self-explanatory. That is the classical imagination; the Parthenon was built for it. It also loves to lose itself in a labyrinth, to surrender to the inextricable. That is the romantic imagination; the *Orlando Furioso* was written for it. But Christian Theology does not cater very well for either.

If Christianity is only a mythology, then I find the mythology I believe in is not the one I like best. I like Greek mythology much better, Irish better still, Norse best of all.

Having thus inspected myself, I next inquire how far my case is peculiar. It does not seem, certainly, to be unique. It is not at all plain that men's imaginations have always delighted most in those pictures of the supernatural which they believed. From the twelfth to the seventeenth century Europe seems to have taken an unfailing delight in classical mythology. If the numbers and the gusto of pictures and poems were to be the criterion of belief, we should judge that those ages were pagan, which we know to be untrue.

It looks as if the confusion between imaginative enjoyment and intellectual assent, of which Christians are accused, is not nearly so common or so easy as some people suppose. Even children, I believe, rarely suffer from it. It pleases their imagination to pretend that they are bears or horses, but I do not remember that one was ever under the least delusion. May it not even be that there is something in belief which is hostile to perfect imaginative enjoyment? The sensitive, cultured atheist seems at times to enjoy the aesthetic trappings of Christianity in a way which the believer can only envy. The modern poets certainly enjoy the Greek gods in a way of which I find no trace in Greek literature. What mythological scenes in ancient literature can compare for a moment with Keats's *Hyperion*? In a certain sense we spoil a mythology for imaginative purposes by believing in it. Fairies are popular in England because we don't think they exist; they are no fun at all in Arran or Connemara.

But I must beware of going too far. I have suggested that belief spoils a system for the imagination "in a certain sense." But not in all senses. If I came to believe in fairies, I should almost certainly lose the particular kind of pleasure which I now get from them when reading the *Midsummer Night's Dream*. But later on, when the believed fairies had settled down as inhabitants of my real universe and had been fully connected with other parts of my thought, a new pleasure might arise. The contemplation of what we take to be real is always, I think, in tolerably sensitive minds, attended with a certain sort of aesthetic satisfaction—a sort which depends precisely on its supposed reality. There is a dignity and poignancy in the bare fact that a thing exists. Thus, as Balfour pointed out in *Theism and Humanism* (a book too little read), there are many historical facts which we should not applaud for any obvious humour or pathos if we supposed them to be inventions; but once we believe them to be real, we have, in addition to our intellectual satisfaction, a certain aesthetic delight in the idea of them. The story of the Trojan War and the story of the Napoleonic Wars both have an aesthetic effect on us. And the effects are different. And this difference does not depend solely on those differences which would make them different as stories if we believed neither. The *kind* of pleasure the Napoleonic Wars give has a certain difference simply because we believe in them. A believed idea *feels* different from an idea that is not believed. And that peculiar flavour of the believed is never, in my experience, without a special sort of imaginative enjoyment. It is therefore quite true that the Christians do enjoy their world picture, aesthetically, once they have accepted it as true. Every man, I believe, enjoys the world picture which he accepts, for the gravity and finality of the actual is itself an aesthetic stimulus. In this sense, Christianity, Life-Force-Worship, Marxism, Freudianism all become "poetries" to their own believers. But this does not mean that their adherents have chosen them for that reason. On the contrary, this kind of poetry is the result, not the cause, of belief. Theology is, in this sense, poetry to me because I believe it; I do not believe it because it is poetry.

The charge that Theology is mere poetry, if it means that Christians believe it because they find it, antecedently to belief, the most poetically attractive of all world pictures, thus seems to me unplausible in the extreme. There may be evidence for such a charge which I do not know of, but such evidence as I do know is against it.

I am not, of course, maintaining that Theology, even before you believe it, is totally bare of aesthetic value. But I do not find it superior in this respect to most of its rivals. Consider for a few moments the enormous aesthetic claim of its chief contemporary rival—what we may loosely call the Scientific Outlook,* the picture of Mr. [H.G.] Wells and the rest. Supposing this to be a myth, is it not one of the finest myths which human imagination has yet produced? The play is preceded by the most austere of all preludes: the infinite void, and matter restlessly moving to bring forth it knows not what. Then, by the millionth millionth chance—what tragic irony—the conditions at one point of space and time bubble up into that tiny fermentation which is the beginning of life. Everything seems to be against the infant hero of our drama—just as everything seems against the youngest son or ill-used stepdaughter at the opening of a fairy tale. But life somehow wins through. With infinite suffering, against all but insuperable obstacles, it spreads, it breeds, it complicates itself, from the amoeba up to the plant, up to the reptile, up to the mammal. We glance briefly at the age of monsters. Dragons prowl the earth, devour one another, and die. Then comes the theme of the younger son and the ugly duckling once more. As the weak, tiny spark of life began amidst the huge hostilities of the inanimate, so now again, amidst the beasts that are far larger and stronger than he, there comes forth a little naked, shivering, cowering creature, shuffling, not

* I am not suggesting that practising scientists believe it as a whole. The delightful name "Wellsianity" (which another member invented during the discussion) would have been much better than "the Scientific Outlook."

yet erect, promising nothing, the product of another millionth millionth chance. Yet somehow he thrives. He becomes the Cave Man with his club and his flints, muttering and growling over his enemies' bones, dragging his screaming mate by her hair (I never could quite make out why), tearing his children to pieces in fierce jealousy till one of them is old enough to tear him, cowering before the horrible gods whom he created in his own image. But these are only growing pains. Wait till the next act. There he is becoming true Man. He learns to master Nature. Science comes and dissipates the superstitions of his infancy. More and more he becomes the controller of his own fate. Passing hastily over the present (for it is a mere nothing by the time scale we are using), you follow him on into the future. See him in the last act, though not the last scene, of this great mystery. A race of demigods now rules the planet—and perhaps more than the planet—for eugenics have made certain that only demigods will be born, and psychoanalysis that none of them shall lose or smirch his divinity, and communism that all which divinity requires shall be ready to their hands. Man has ascended his throne. Henceforward he has nothing to do but to practise virtue, to grow in wisdom, to be happy. And now, mark the final stroke of genius. If the myth stopped at that point, it might be a little bathetic. It would lack the highest grandeur of which human imagination is capable. The last scene reverses all. We have the Twilight of the Gods. All this time, silently, unceasingly, out of all reach of human power, Nature, the old enemy, has been steadily gnawing away. The sun will cool—all suns will cool—the whole universe will run down. Life (every form of life) will be banished, without hope of return, from every inch of infinite space. All ends in nothingness, and "universal darkness covers all." The pattern of the myth thus becomes one of the noblest we can conceive. It is the pattern of many Elizabethan tragedies, where the protagonist's career can be represented by a slowly ascending and then rapidly falling curve, with its highest point in Act IV. You see him climbing up and up, then blazing in his bright meridian, then finally overwhelmed in ruin.

Such a world drama appeals to every part of us. The early struggles of the hero (a theme delightfully doubled, played first by life, and then by man) appeal to our generosity. His future exaltation gives scope to a reasonable optimism, for the tragic close is so very distant that you need not often think of it—we work with millions of years. And the tragic close itself just gives that irony, that grandeur, which calls forth our defiance, and without which all the rest might cloy. There is a beauty in this myth which well deserves better poetic handling than it has yet received; I hope some great genius will yet crystallise it before the incessant stream of philosophic change carries it all away. I am speaking, of course, of the beauty it has whether you believe it or not. There I can speak from experience, for I, who believe less than half of what it tells me about the past, and less than nothing of what it tells me about the future, am deeply moved when I contemplate it. The only other story—unless, indeed, it is an embodiment of the same story—which similarly moves me is the *Nibelung's Ring. Enden sah ich die Welt*.

We cannot, therefore, turn down Theology, sim-

ply because it does not avoid being poetical. All
world views yield poetry to those who believe them
by the mere fact of being believed. And nearly all
have certain poetical merits whether you believe
them or not. This is what we should expect. Man
is a poetical animal and touches nothing which
he does not adorn.

There are, however, two other lines of thought
which might lead us to call Theology a mere poetry,
and these I must now consider. In the first place, it
certainly contains elements similar to those which
we find in many early, and even savage, religions.
And those elements in the early religions may now
seem to us to be poetical. The question here is
rather complicated. We now regard the death and
return of Balder as a poetical idea, a myth. We are
invited to infer thence that the death and resurrection of Christ is a poetical idea, a myth. But we are
not really starting with the *datum* "both are poetical" and thence arguing "therefore both are false."
Part of the poetical aroma which hangs about
Balder is, I believe, due to the fact that we have
already come to disbelieve in him. So that disbelief,
not poetical experience, is the real starting point
of the argument. But this is perhaps an over-
subtlety, certainly a subtlety, and I will leave it on
one side.

What light is really thrown on the truth or falsehood of Christian Theology by the occurrence of
similar ideas in Pagan religion? I think the answer
was very well given a fortnight ago by Mr. Brown.
Supposing, for purposes of argument, that Christianity is true; then it could avoid all coincidence
with other religions only on the supposition that
all other religions are one hundred percent errone-

ous. To which, you remember, Professor H. H. Price replied by agreeing with Mr. Brown and saying, "Yes. From these resemblances you may conclude not 'so much the worse for the Christians' but 'so much the better for the Pagans.' " The truth is that the resemblances tell nothing either for or against the truth of Christian Theology. If you start from the assumption that the Theology is false, the resemblances are quite consistent with that assumption. One would expect creatures of the same sort, faced with the same universe, to make the same false guess more than once. But if you start with the assumption that the Theology is true, the resemblances fit in equally well. Theology, while saying that a special illumination has been vouchsafed to Christians and (earlier) to Jews, also says that there is some divine illumination vouchsafed to all men. The Divine light, we are told, "lighteneth every man." We should, therefore, expect to find in the imagination of great Pagan teachers and myth makers some glimpse of that theme which we believe to be the very plot of the whole cosmic story—the theme of incarnation, death, and rebirth. And the differences between the Pagan Christs (Balder, Osiris, etc.) and the Christ Himself is much what we should expect to find. The Pagan stories are all about someone dying and rising, either every year, or else nobody knows where and nobody knows when. The Christian story is about a historical personage, whose execution can be dated pretty accurately, under a named Roman magistrate, and with whom the society that He founded is in a continous relation down to the present day. It is not the difference between falsehood and truth. It is the difference between a real event on the one hand and dim dreams or premonitions of that same event on the other. It is like watching something come gradually into focus; first it hangs in the clouds of myth and ritual, vast and vague, then it condenses, grows hard and in a sense small, as a historical event in first century Palestine. This gradual focussing goes on even inside the Christian tradition itself. The earliest stratum of the Old Testament contains many truths in a form which I take to be legendary, or even mythical—hanging in the clouds, but gradually the truth condenses, becomes more and more historical. From things like Noah's Ark or the sun standing still upon Ajalon, you come down to the court memoirs of King David. Finally you reach the New Testament and history reigns supreme, and the Truth is incarnate. And "incarnate" is here more than a metaphor. It is not an accidental resemblance that what, from the point of view of being, is stated in the form "God became Man," should involve, from the point of view of human knowledge, the statement "Myth became Fact." The essential meaning of all things came down from the "heaven" of myth to the "earth" of history. In so doing, it partly emptied itself of its glory, as Christ emptied Himself of His glory to be Man. That is the real explanation of the fact that Theology, far from defeating its rivals by a superior poetry, is, in a superficial but quite real sense, less poetical than they. That is why the New Testament is, in the same sense, less poetical than the Old. Have you not often felt in Church, if the first lesson is some great passage, that the second lesson is somehow small by comparison—almost, if one might say so, humdrum? So it is and so it must be. That is the humiliation of myth into fact, of

God into Man; what is everywhere and always, imageless and ineffable, only to be glimpsed in dream and symbol and the acted poetry of ritual becomes small, solid—no bigger than a man who can lie asleep in a rowing boat on the Lake of Galilee. You may say that this, after all, is a still deeper poetry. I will not contradict you. The humiliation leads to a greater glory. But the humiliation of God and the shrinking or condensation of the myth as it becomes fact are also quite real.

I have just mentioned symbol, and that brings me to the last head under which I will consider the charge of "mere poetry." Theology certainly shares with poetry the use of metaphorical or symbolical language. The first Person of the Trinity is not the Father of the Second in a physical sense. The Second Person did not come "down" to earth in the same sense as a parachutist, nor reascend into the sky like a balloon, nor did He literally sit at the right hand of the Father. Why, then, does Christianity talk as if all these things did happen? The agnostic thinks that it does so because those who founded it were quite naïvely ignorant and believed all these statements literally, and we later Christians have gone on using the same language through timidity and conservatism. We are often invited, in Professor [H. H.] Price's words, to throw away the shell and retain the kernel.

There are two questions involved here.

1. What did the early Christians believe? Did they believe that God really has a material palace in the sky and that He received His Son in a decorated state chair placed a little to the right of His own?—or did they not? The answer is that the alternative we are offering them was probably

never present to their minds at all. As soon as it was present, we know quite well which side of the fence they came down. As soon as the issue of Anthropomorphism was explicitly before the Church in, I think, the second century, Anthropomorphism was condemned. The Church knew the answer (that God has no body and therefore couldn't sit in a chair) as soon as it knew the question. But till the question was raised, of course, people believed neither the one answer nor the other. There is no more tiresome error in the history of thought than to try to sort our ancestors on to this or that side of a distinction which was not in their minds at all. You are asking a question to which no answer exists. It is very probable that most (almost certainly not all) of the first generation of Christians never thought of their faith without anthropomorphic imagery, and that they were not explicitly conscious, as a modern would be, that it *was* mere imagery. But this does not in the least mean that the essence of their belief was concerned with details about a celestial throne room. That was not what they valued, or what they were prepared to die for. Any one of them who went to Alexandria and got a philosophical education would have recognised the imagery at once for what it was, and would not have felt that his belief had been altered in any way that mattered. My mental picture of an Oxford college, before I saw one, was very different from the reality in physical details. But this did not mean that when I came to Oxford I found my general conception of what a college means to have been a delusion. The physical pictures had inevitably accompanied my thinking, but they had never been what I was chiefly interested in, and much of my thinking had been correct in spite of them. What you think is one thing; what you imagine while you are thinking is another.

The earliest Christians were not so much like a man who mistakes the shell for the kernel as like a man carrying a nut which he hasn't yet cracked. The moment it is cracked, he knows which part to throw away. Till then he holds on to the nut, not because he is a fool but because he isn't.

2. We are invited to restate our belief in a form free from metaphor and symbol. The reason we don't is that we can't. We can, if you like, say "God entered history" instead of saying "God came down to earth." But, of course, "entered" is just as metaphorical as "came down." You have only substituted horizontal or undefined movement for vertical movement. We can make our language duller; we cannot make it less metaphorical. We can make the pictures more prosaic; we cannot be less pictorial. Nor are we Christians alone in this disability. Here is a sentence from a celebrated anti-Christian writer, Dr. I. A. Richards.* "Only that part of the cause of a mental event which takes effect through incoming (sensory) impulses or through effects of past sensory impulses can be said to be thereby known. The reservation no doubt involves complications." Dr. Richards does not mean that the part of the cause "takes" effect in the literal sense of the word *takes*, nor that it does so *through* a sensory impulse as you could take a parcel *through* a doorway. In the second sentence "The reservation involves complications," he does not mean that an act of defending, or a seat booked in a train, or an

* *Principles of Literary Criticism* (1924), Chap. XI.

American park, really sets about rolling or folding or curling up a set of coilings or rollings up. In other words, all language about things other than physical objects is necessarily metaphorical.

For all these reasons, then, I think (though we knew even before Freud that the heart is deceitful) that those who accept Theology are not necessarily being guided by taste rather than reason. The picture so often painted of Christians huddling together on an ever narrower strip of beach while the incoming tide of "Science" mounts higher and higher corresponds to nothing in my own experience. That grand myth which I asked you to admire a few minutes ago is not for me a hostile novelty breaking in on my traditional beliefs. On the contrary, that cosmology is what I started from. Deepening distrust and final abandonment of it long preceded my conversion to Christianity. Long before I believed Theology to be true I had already decided that the popular scientific picture at any rate was false. One absolutely central inconsistency ruins it; it is the one we touched on a fortnight ago.* The whole picture professes to depend on inferences from observed facts. Unless inference is valid, the whole picture disappears. Unless we can be sure that reality in the remotest nebula or the remotest part obeys the thought laws of the human scientist here and now in his laboratory—in other words, unless Reason is an absolute—all is in ruins. Yet those who ask me to believe this world picture also ask me to believe that Reason is simply the unforeseen and unintended by-product of mindless

---

* When, on 30 October 1944, Dr. David Edwards read to the Socratic Club a paper entitled, "Is Belief in a Personal God Compatible with Modern Scientific Knowledge?"—ed.

matter at one stage of its endless and aimless becoming. Here is flat contradiction. They ask me at the same moment to accept a conclusion and to discredit the only testimony on which that conclusion can be based. The difficulty is to me a fatal one; and the fact that when you put it to many scientists, far from having an answer, they seem not even to understand what the difficulty is, assures me that I have not found a mare's nest but detected a radical disease in their whole mode of thought from the very beginning. The man who has once understood the situation is compelled henceforth to regard the scientific cosmology as being, in principle, a myth; though no doubt a great many true particulars have been worked into it.*

After that it is hardly worth noticing minor difficulties. Yet these are many and serious. The Bergsonian critique of orthodox Darwinism is not easy to answer. More disquieting still is Professor D. M. S. Watson's defence. "Evolution itself," he wrote,† "is accepted by zoologists not because it has been observed to occur or . . . can be proved by logically coherent evidence to be true, but because the only alternative, special creation, is clearly incredible." Has it come to that? Does the whole vast structure of modern naturalism depend not on positive evidence but simply on an *a priori* metaphysical prejudice? Was it devised not to get in facts but to keep out God? Even, however, if Evolution in the

---

* It is not irrelevant, in considering the mythical character of this cosmology, to notice that the two great imaginative expressions of it are *earlier* than the evidence: Keat's *Hyperion* and the *Nibelung's Ring* are pre-Darwinian works.

† Quoted in "Science and the B.B.C.," *Nineteenth Century,* April 1943.

strict biological sense has some better grounds than Professor Watson suggests—and I can't help thinking it must—we should distinguish Evolution in this strict sense from what may be called the universal evolutionism of modern thought. By universal evolutionism I mean the belief that the very formula of universal process is from imperfect to perfect, from small beginnings to great endings, from the rudimentary to the elaborate, the belief which makes people find it natural to think that morality springs from savage taboos, adult sentiment from infantile sexual maladjustments, thought from instinct, mind from matter, organic from inorganic, cosmos from chaos. This is perhaps the deepest habit of mind in the contemporary world. It seems to me immensely unplausible, because it makes the general course of nature so very unlike those parts of nature we can observe. You remember the old puzzle as to whether the owl came from the egg or the egg from the owl. The modern acquiescence in universal evolutionism is a kind of optical illusion, produced by attending exclusively to the owl's emergence from the egg. We are taught from childhood to notice how the perfect oak grows from the acorn and to forget that the acorn itself was dropped by a perfect oak. We are reminded constantly that the adult human being was an embryo, never that the life of the embryo came from two adult human beings. We love to notice that the express engine of today is the descendant of the "Rocket"; we do not equally remember that the "Rocket" springs not from some even more rudimentary engine, but from something much more perfect and complicated than itself—namely, a man of genius. The obviousness or naturalness which most people seem to find in the idea of emergent evolution thus seems to be a pure hallucination.

On these grounds and others like them one is driven to think that whatever else may be true, the popular scientific cosmology at any rate is certainly not. I left that ship not at the call of poetry but because I thought it could not keep afloat. Something like philosophical idealism or Theism must, at the very worst, be less untrue than that. And idealism turned out, when you took it seriously, to be disguised Theism. And once you accepted Theism, you could not ignore the claims of Christ. And when you examined them it appeared to me that you could adopt no middle position. Either He was a lunatic, or God. And He was not a lunatic.

I was taught at school, when I had done a sum, to "prove my answer." The proof or verification of my Christian answer to the cosmic sun is this. When I accept Theology I may find difficulties, at this point or that, in harmonising it with some particular truths which are imbedded in the mythical cosmology derived from science. But I can get in, or allow for, science as a whole. Granted that Reason is prior to matter and that the light of that primal Reason illuminates finite minds, I can understand how men should come, by observation and inference, to know a lot about the universe they live in. If, on the other hand, I swallow the scientific cosmology as a whole, then not only can I not fit in Christianity, but I cannot even fit in science. If minds are wholly dependent on brains, and brains on biochemistry, and biochemistry (in the long run) on the meaningless flux of the atoms, I cannot understand how the thought of those minds should have any more significance than the sound of the wind in the trees. And this is to me the final test. This is how I distinguish dreaming and waking. When I am awake I can, in some degree, account for and study my dream. The dragon that pursued me last night can be fitted into my waking world. I know that there are such things are dreams; I know that I had eaten an indigestible dinner; I know that a man of my reading might be expected to dream of dragons. But while in the nightmare I could not have fitted in my waking experience. The waking world is judged more real because it can thus contain the dreaming world; the dreaming world is judged less real because it cannot contain the waking one. For the same reason I am certain that in passing from the scientific points of view to the theological, I have passed from dream to waking. Christian theology can fit in science, art, morality, and the sub-Christian religions. The scientific point of view cannot fit in any of these things, not even science itself. I believe in Christianity as I believe that the Sun has risen, not only because I see it, but because by it I see everything else.

THE INNER RING

May I read you a few lines from Tolstoi's *War and Peace*?

When Boris entered the room, Prince Andrey was listening to an old general, wearing his decorations, who was reporting something to Prince Andrey, with an expression of soldierly servility on his purple face. "Alright. Please wait!" he said to the general, speaking in Russian with the French accent which he used when he spoke with contempt. The moment he noticed Boris he stopped listening to the general who trotted imploringly after him and begged to be heard, while Prince Andrey turned to Boris with a cheerful smile and a nod of the head. Boris now clearly understood—what he had already guessed—that side by side with the system of discipline and subordination which were laid down in the Army Regulations, there existed a different and a more real system—the system which compelled a tightly laced general with a purple face to wait respectfully for his turn while a mere captain like Prince Andrey chatted with a mere second lieutenant like Boris. Boris decided at once that he would be guided not by the official system but by this other unwritten system.*

When you invite a middle-aged moralist to address you, I suppose I must conclude, however unlikely the conclusion seems, that you have a taste for middle-aged moralising. I shall do my best to gratify it. I shall in fact give you advice about the world

* Part III, Chapter 9.

in which you are going to live. I do not mean by this that I am going to attempt a talk on what are called current affairs. You probably know quite as much about them as I do. I am not going to tell you— except in a form so general that you will hardly recognise it—what part you ought to play in post-war reconstruction. It is not, in fact, very likely that any of you will be able, in the next ten years, to make any direct contribution to the peace or prosperity of Europe. You will be busy finding jobs, getting married, acquiring facts. I am going to do something more old-fashioned than you perhaps expected. I am going to give advice. I am going to issue warnings. Advice and warnings about things which are so perennial that no one calls them "current affairs."

And of course everyone knows what a middle-aged moralist of my type warns his juniors against. He warns them against the World, the Flesh, and the Devil. But one of this trio will be enough to deal with today. The Devil I shall leave strictly alone. The association between him and me in the public mind has already gone quite as deep as I wish; in some quarters it has already reached the level of confusion, if not of identification. I begin to realise the truth of the old proverb that he who sups with that formidable host needs a long spoon. As for the Flesh, you must be very abnormal young people if you do not know quite as much about it as I do. But on the World I think I have something to say.

In the passage I have just read from Tolstoi, the young second lieutenant Boris Dubretskoi discovers that there exist in the army two different systems or hierarchies. The one is printed in some little red book and anyone can easily read it up. It also remains constant. A general is always superior to a colonel and a colonel to a captain. The other is not printed anywhere. Nor is it even a formally organised secret society with rules which you would be told after you had been admitted. You are never formally and explicitly admitted by anyone. You discover gradually, in almost indefinable ways, that it exists and that you are outside it, and then later, perhaps, that you are inside it. There are what correspond to passwords, but they too are spontaneous and informal. A particular slang, the use of particular nicknames, an allusive manner of conversation are the marks. But it is not constant. It is not easy, even at a given moment, to say who is inside and who is outside. Some people are obviously in and some are obviously out, but there are always several on the border line. And if you come back to the same divisional headquarters, or brigade headquarters, or the same regiment, or even the same company after six weeks' absence, you may find this second hierarchy quite altered. There are no formal admissions or expulsions. People think they are in it after they have in fact been pushed out of it, or before they have been allowed in; this provides great amusement for those who are really inside. It has no fixed name. The only certain rule is that the insiders and outsiders call it by different names. From inside it may be designated, in simple cases, by mere enumeration; it may be called "you and Tony and me." When it is very secure and comparatively stable in membership, it calls itself "we." When it has to be suddenly expanded to meet a particular emergency, it calls itself "all the sensible people at this place." From outside, if you have despaired of getting into it, you call it "that gang" or "they" or "so-and-so and his set" or "the Caucus" or "the Inner Ring." If you are a candidate for admission, you probably don't call it anything. To discuss it with the other outsiders would make you feel outside yourself. And to mention it in talking to the man who is inside, and who may help you in if this present conversation goes well, would be madness.

Badly as I may have described it, I hope you will all have recognised the thing I am describing. Not, of course, that you have been in the Russian Army or perhaps in any army. But you have met the phenomenon of an Inner Ring. You discovered one in your house at school before the end of the first term. And when you had climbed up to somewhere near it by the end of your second year, perhaps you discovered that within the Ring there was a Ring yet more inner, which in its turn was the fringe of the great school Ring to which the house Rings were only satellites. It is even possible that the School Ring was almost in touch with a Masters' Ring. You were begining, in fact, to pierce through the skins of the onion. And here, too, at your university—shall I be wrong in assuming that at this very moment, invisible to me, there are several rings —independent systems or concentric rings—present in this room? And I can assure you that in whatever hospital, inn of court, diocèse, school, business, or college you arrive after going down, you will find the Rings—what Tolstoi calls the second or unwritten systems.

All this is rather obvious. I wonder whether you will say the same of my next step, which is this. I believe that in all men's lives at certain periods, and in many men's lives at all periods between infancy and extreme old age, one of the most dominant elements is the desire to be inside the local Ring and the terror of being left outside. This desire, in one of its forms, has indeed had ample justice done to it in literature. I mean, in the form of snobbery. Victorian fiction is full of characters who are hagridden by the desire to get inside that particular Ring which is, or was, called Society. But it must be clearly understood that "Society," in that sense of the word, is merely one of a hundred Rings and snobbery, therefore, only one form of the longing to be inside. People who believe themselves to be free, and indeed are free, from snobbery, and who read satires on snobbery with tranquil superiority, may be devoured by the desire in another form. It may be the very intensity of their desire to enter some quite different Ring which renders them immune from the allurements of high life. An invitation from a duchess would be very cold comfort to a man smarting under the sense of exclusion from some artistic or communist côterie. Poor man—it is not large, lighted rooms, or champagne, or even scandals about peers and Cabinet Ministers that he wants; it is the sacred little attic or studio, the heads bent together, the fog of tobacco smoke, and the delicious knowledge that we—we four or five all huddled beside this stove—are the people who *know*. Often the desire conceals itself so well that we hardly recognise the pleasures of fruition. Men tell not only their wives but themselves that it is a hardship to stay late at the office or the school on some bit of important extra work which they have been let in for because they and So-and-so and the two others are the only people left in the place who really know how things are run. But it is not quite true. It is a terrible bore, of course, when old Fatty Smithson draws you aside and whispers, "Look here, we've got to get you in on this examination somehow" or "Charles and I saw at once that you've got to be on this committee." A terrible bore . . . ah, but how much more terrible if you were left out! It is tiring and unhealthy to lose your Saturday afternoons, but to have them free because you don't matter, that is much worse.

Freud would say, no doubt, that the whole thing is a subterfuge of the sexual impulse. I wonder whether the shoe is not sometimes on the other foot. I wonder whether, in ages of promiscuity, many a virginity has not been lost less in obedience to Venus than in obedience to the lure of the caucus. For, of course, when promiscuity is the fashion, the chaste are outsiders. They are ignorant of something that other people know. They are uninitiated. And as for lighter matters, the number who first smoked or first got drunk for a similar reason is probably very large.

I must now make a distinction. I am not going to say that the existence of Inner Rings is an evil. It is certainly unavoidable. There must be confidential discussions, and it is not only not a bad thing, it is (in itself) a good thing that personal friendship should grow up between those who work together. And it is perhaps impossible that the official hierarchy of any organisation should quite coincide with its actual workings. If the wisest and most energetic people invariably held the highest posts, it might coincide; since they often do not, there must be people in high positions who are really deadweights and people in lower positions who are more important than their rank and seniority would lead you to suppose. In that way the second, unwritten system is bound to grow up. It is necessary, and perhaps it is not a necessary evil. But the desire which draws us into Inner Rings is another matter. A thing may be morally neutral and yet the desire for that thing may be dangerous. As Byron has said:

> Sweet is a legacy, and passing sweet
> The unexpected death of some old lady.

The painless death of a pious relative at an advanced age is not an evil. But an earnest desire for her death on the part of her heirs is not reckoned a proper feeling, and the law frowns on even the gentlest attempt to expedite her departure. Let Inner Rings be an unavoidable and even an innocent feature of life, though certainly not a beautiful one; but what of our longing to enter them, our anguish when we are excluded, and the kind of pleasure we feel when we get in?

I have no right to make assumptions about the degree to which any of you may already be compromised. I must not assume that you have ever first neglected, and finally shaken off, friends whom you really loved and who might have lasted you a lifetime, in order to court the friendship of those who appeared to you more important, more esoteric. I must not ask whether you have ever derived actual pleasure from the loneliness and humiliation of the outsiders after you yourself were in; whether you have talked to fellow members of the Ring in the presence of outsiders simply in order that the outsiders might envy; whether the means whereby, in your days of probation, you propitiated the Inner

Ring were always wholly admirable. I will ask only one question—and it is, of course, a rhetorical question which expects no answer. In the whole of your life as you now remember it, has the desire to be on the right side of that invisible line ever prompted you to any act or word on which, in the cold small hours of a wakeful night, you can look back with satisfaction? If so, your case is more fortunate than most.

But I said I was going to give advice, and advice should deal with the future, not the past. I have hinted at the past only to awake you to what I believe to be the real nature of human life. I don't believe that the economic motive and the erotic motive account for everything that goes on in what we moralists call the World. Even if you add Ambition, I think the picture is still incomplete. The lust for the esoteric, the longing to be inside, take many forms which are not easily recognisable as Ambition. We hope, no doubt, for tangible profits from every Inner Ring we penetrate: power, money, liberty to break rules, avoidance of routine duties, evasion of discipline. But all these would not satisfy us if we did not get in addition the delicious sense of secret intimacy. It is no doubt a great convenience to know that we need fear no official reprimands from our official senior because he is old Percy, a fellow member of our Ring. But we don't value the intimacy only for the sake of convenience; quite equally we value the convenience as a proof of the intimacy.

My main purpose in this address is simply to convince you that this desire is one of the great permanent mainsprings of human action. It is one of the factors which go to make up the world as we know it—this whole pell-mell of struggle, competition, confusion, graft, disappointment, and advertisement, and if it is one of the permanent mainsprings, then you may be quite sure of this. Unless you take measures to prevent it, this desire is going to be one of the chief motives of your life, from the first day on which you enter your profession until the day when you are too old to care. That will be the natural thing—the life that will come to you of its own accord. Any other kind of life, if you lead it, will be the result of conscious and continuous effort. If you do nothing about it, if you drift with the stream, you will in fact be an "inner ringer." I don't say you'll be a successful one; that's as may be. But whether by pining and moping outside Rings that you can never enter, or by passing triumphantly further and further in—one way or the other you will be that kind of man.

I have already made it fairly clear that I think it better for you not to be that kind of man. But you may have an open mind on the question. I will therefore suggest two reasons for thinking as I do.

It would be polite and charitable and, in view of your age, reasonable, too, to suppose that none of you is yet a scoundrel. On the other hand, by the mere law of averages (I am saying nothing against free will) it is almost certain that at least two or three of you before you die will have become something very like scoundrels. There must be in this room the makings of at least that number of unscrupulous, treacherous, ruthless egotists. The choice is still before you, and I hope you will not take my hard words about your possible future characters as a token of disrespect to your present characters. And the prophecy I make is this. To nine out of ten of you the choice which could lead to scoundrelism will come, when it does come, in no very dramatic colours. Obviously bad men, obviously threatening or bribing, will almost certainly not appear. Over a drink or a cup of coffee, disguised as a triviality and sandwiched between two jokes, from the lips of a man, or woman, whom you have recently been getting to know rather better and whom you hope to know better still—just at the moment when you are most anxious not to appear crude, or naïf or a prig—the hint will come. It will be the hint of something which is not quite in accordance with the technical rules of fair play; something which the public, the ignorant, romantic public, would never understand; something which even the outsiders in your own profession are apt to make a fuss about, but something, says your new friend, which "we"—and at the word "we" you try not to blush for mere pleasure—something "we always do." And you will be drawn in, if you are drawn in, not by desire for gain or ease, but simply because at that moment, when the cup was so near your lips, you cannot bear to be thrust back again into the cold outer world. It would be so terrible to see the other man's face—that genial, confidential, delightfully sophisticated face—turn suddenly cold and contemptuous, to know that you had been tried for the Inner Ring and rejected. And then, if you are drawn in, next week it will be something a little further from the rules, and next year something further still, but all in the jolliest, friendliest spirit. It may end in a crash, a scandal, and penal servitude; it may end in millions, a peerage, and giving the prizes at your old school. But you will be a scoundrel.

That is my first reason. Of all passions the passion for the Inner Ring is most skillful in making a man who is not yet a very bad man do very bad things.

My second reason is this. The torture allotted to the Danaids in the classical underworld, that of attempting to fill sieves with water, is the symbol not of one vice but of all vices. It is the very mark of a perverse desire that it seeks what is not to be had. The desire to be inside the invisible line illustrates this rule. As long as you are governed by that desire you will never get what you want. You are trying to peel an onion; if you succeed there will be nothing left. Until you conquer the fear of being an outsider, an outsider you will remain.

This is surely very clear when you come to think of it. If you want to be made free of a certain circle for some wholesome reason—if, say, you want to join a musical society because you really like music —then there is a possibility of satisfaction. You may find yourself playing in a quartet and you may enjoy it. But if all you want is to be in the know, your pleasure will be short-lived. The circle cannot have from within the charm it had from outside. By the very act of admiring you it has lost its magic. Once the first novelty is worn off, the members of this circle will be no more interesting than your old friends. Why should they be? You were not looking for virtue or kindness or loyalty or humour or learning or wit or any of the things that can be really enjoyed. You merely wanted to be "in." And that is a pleasure that cannot last. As soon as your new associates have been staled to you by custom, you will be looking for another Ring.

The rainbow's end will still be ahead of you. The old Ring will now be only the drab background for your endeavour to enter the new one.

And you will always find them hard to enter, for a reason you very well know. You yourself, once you are in, want to make it hard for the next entrant, just as those who are already in made it hard for you. Naturally. In any wholesome group of people which holds together for a good purpose, the exclusions are in a sense accidental. Three or four people who are together for the sake of some piece of work exclude others because there is work only for so many or because the others can't in fact do it. Your little musical group limits its numbers because the rooms they meet in are only so big. But your genuine Inner Ring exists for exclusion. There'd be no fun if there were no outsiders. The invisible line would have no meaning unless most people were on the wrong side of it. Exclusion is no accident; it is the essence.

The quest of the Inner Ring will break your hearts unless you break it. But if you break it, a surprising result will follow. If in your working hours you make the work your end, you will presently find yourself all unawares inside the only circle in your profession that really matters. You will be one of the sound craftsmen, and other sound craftsmen will know it. This group of craftsmen will by no means coincide with the Inner Ring or the Important People or the People in the Know. It will not shape that professional policy or work up that professional influence which fights for the profession as a whole against the public, nor will it lead to those periodic scandals and crises which the Inner Ring produces. But it will do those things which that profession exists to do and will in the long run be responsible for all the respect which that profession in fact enjoys and which the speeches and advertisements cannot maintain. And if in your spare time you consort simply with the people you like, you will again find that you have come unawares to a real inside, that you are indeed snug and safe at the centre of something which, seen from without, would look exactly like an Inner Ring. But the difference is that its secrecy is accidental, and its exclusiveness a by-product, and no one was led thither by the lure of the esoteric, for it is only four or five people who like one another meeting to do things that they like. This is friendship. Aristotle placed it among the virtues. It causes perhaps half of all the happiness in the world, and no Inner Ringer can ever have it.

We are told in Scripture that those who ask get. That is true, in senses I can't now explore. But in another sense there is much truth in the schoolboy's principle "them as asks shan't have." To a young person, just entering on adult life, the world seems full of "insides," full of delightful intimacies and confidentialities, and he desires to enter them. But if he follows that desire he will reach no "inside" that is worth reaching. The true road lies in quite another direction. It is like the house in *Alice Through the Looking Glass.*

MEMBERSHIP

No Christian and, indeed, no historian could accept the epigram which defines religion as "what a man does with his solitude." It was one of the Wesleys, I think, who said that the New Testament knows nothing of solitary religion. We are forbidden to neglect the assembling of ourselves together. Christianity is already institutional in the earliest of its documents. The Church is the Bride of Christ. We are members of one another.

In our own age the idea that religion belongs to our private life—that it is, in fact, an occupation for the individual's hour of leisure—is at once paradoxical, dangerous, and natural. It is paradoxical because this exaltation of the individual in the religious field springs up in an age when collectivism is ruthlessly defeating the individual in every other field. I see this even in a university. When I first went to Oxford the typical undergraduate society consisted of a dozen men, who knew one another intimately, hearing a paper by one of their own number in a small sitting-room and hammering out their problem till one or two in the morning. Before the war the typical undergraduate society had come to be a mixed audience of one or two hundred students assembled in a public hall to hear a lecture from some visiting celebrity. Even on those rare occasions when a modern undergraduate is not attending some such society he is seldom engaged in those solitary walks, or walks with a single companion, which built the minds of the previous generations. He lives in a crowd; caucus has replaced friendship. And this tendency not only exists both within and without the university, but is often approved. There is a crowd of busybodies, self-appointed masters of ceremonies, whose life is devoted to destroying solitude wherever solitude still exists. They call it "taking the young people out of themselves," or "waking them up," or "overcoming their apathy." If an Augustine, a Vaughan, a Traherne, or a Wordsworth should be born in the modern world, the leaders of a youth organization would soon cure him. If a really good home, such as the home of Alcinous and Arete in the *Odyssey* or the Rostovs in *War and Peace* or any of Charlotte M. Yonge's families, existed today, it would be denounced as *bourgeois* and every engine of destruction would be levelled against it. And even where the planners fail and someone is left physically by himself, the wireless has seen to it that he will be—in a sense not intended by Scipio—never less alone than when alone. We live, in fact, in a world starved for solitude, silence, and privacy, and therefore starved for meditation and true friendship.

That religion should be relegated to solitude in such an age is, then, paradoxical. But it is also dangerous for two reasons. In the first place, when the modern world says to us aloud, "You may be religious when you are alone," it adds under its breath, "and I will see to it that you never are alone." To make Christianity a private affair while banishing all privacy is to relegate it to the rainbow's end or the Greek calends. That is one of the enemy's stratagems. In the second place, there is the danger that real Christians who know that Christianity is not a solitary affair may react against that error by simply transporting into our spiritual life that same collectivism which has already conquered our secular life. That is the enemy's other stratagem. Like a good chess player, he is always trying to manoeuvre you into a position where you can save your castle only by losing your bishop. In order to avoid the trap we must insist that though the private conception of Christianity is an error, it is a profoundly natural one and is clumsily attempting to guard a great truth. Behind it is the obvious feeling that our modern collectivism is an outrage upon human nature and that from this, as from all other evils, God will be our shield and buckler.

This feeling is just. As personal and private life is lower than participation in the Body of Christ, so the collective life is lower than the personal and private life and has no value save in its service. The secular community, since it exists for our natural good and not for our supernatural, has no higher end than to facilitate and safeguard the family, and friendship, and solitude. To be happy at home, said Johnson, is the end of all human endeavour. As long as we are thinking only of natural values we must say that the sun looks down on nothing half so good as a household laughing together over a meal, or two friends talking over a pint of beer, or a man alone reading a book that interests him; and that all economic, politics, laws, armies, and institutions, save insofar as they prolong and multiply such scenes, are a mere ploughing the sand and sowing the ocean, a meaningless vanity and vexation of spirit. Collective activities are, of course, necessary, but this is the end to which they are necessary. Great sacrifices of this private happiness by those who have it may be necessary in order that it may be more widely distributed. All may have to be a little hungry in order that none may starve. But do not let us mistake necessary evils for good. The mistake is easily made. Fruit has to be tinned if it is to be transported and has to lose thereby some of its good qualities. But one meets people who have learned actually to prefer the tinned fruit to the fresh. A sick society must think much about politics, as a sick man must think much about his digestion; to ignore the subject may be fatal cowardice for the one as for the other. But if either comes to regard it as the natural food of the mind—if either forgets that we think of such things only in order to be able to think of something else —then what was undertaken for the sake of health has become itself a new and deadly disease.

There is, in fact, a fatal tendency in all human activities for the means to encroach upon the very ends which they were intended to serve. Thus money comes to hinder the exchange of commodities, and rules of art to hamper genius, and examinations to prevent young men from becoming learned. It does not, unfortunately, always follow that the encroaching means can be dispensed with. I think it probable that the collectivism of our life is necessary and will increase, and I think that our only safeguard against its deathly properties is in a Christian life, for we were promised that we could handle serpents and drink deadly things and yet live. That is the truth behind the erroneous definition of religion with which we started. Where

it went wrong was in opposing to the collective
mass mere solitude. The Christian is called not to
individualism but to membership in the mystical
body. A consideration of the differences between
the secular collective and the mystical body is therefore the first step to understanding how Christianity
without being individualistic can yet counteract
collectivism.

At the outset we are hampered by a difficulty of
language. The very word *membership* is of Christian
origin, but it has been taken over by the world and
emptied of all meaning. In any book on logic you
may see the expression "members of a class." It must
be most emphatically stated that the items or particulars included in a homogeneous class are almost
the reverse of what St. Paul meant by *members*.
By *members* (μέλη) he meant what we should call
organs, things essentially different from, and complementary to, one another, things differing not
only in structure and function but also in dignity.
Thus, in a club, the committee as a whole and the
servants as a whole may both properly be regarded
as "members"; what we should call the members
of the club are merely units. A row of identically
dressed and identically trained soldiers set side by
side, or a number of citizens listed as voters in a
constituency are not members of anything in the
Pauline sense. I am afraid that when we describe
a man as "a member of the Church" we usually
mean nothing Pauline; we mean only that he is a
unit—that he is one more specimen of some kind
of things as X and Y and Z. How true membership
in a body differs from inclusion in a collective
may be seen in the structure of a family. The grandfather, the parents, the grown-up son, the child, the

dog, and the cat are true members (in the organic sense), precisely because they are not members or units of a homogeneous class. They are not interchangeable. Each person is almost a species in himself. The mother is not simply a different person from the daughter; she is a different kind of person. The grown-up brother is not simply one unit in the class children; he is a separate estate of the realm. The father and grandfather are almost as different as the cat and the dog. If you subtract any one member, you have not simply reduced the family in number; you have inflicted an injury on its structure. Its unity is a unity of unlikes, almost of incommensurables.

A dim perception of the richness inherent in this kind of unity is one reason why we enjoy a book like *The Wind in the Willows*; a trio such as Rat, Mole, and Badger symbolises the extreme differentiation of persons in harmonious union, which we know intuitively to be our true refuge both from solitude and from the collective. The affection between such oddly matched couples as Dick Swiveller and the Marchioness, or Mr. Pickwick and Sam Weller pleases in the same way. That is why the modern notion that children should call their parents by their Christian names is so perverse. For this is an effort to ignore the difference in kind which makes for real organic unity. They are trying to inoculate the child with the preposterous view that one's mother is simply a fellow citizen like anyone else, to make it ignorant of what all men know and insensible to what all men feel. They are trying to drag the featureless repetitions of the collective into the fuller and more concrete world of the family.

A convict has a number instead of a name. That is the collective idea carried to its extreme. But a man in his own house may also lose his name, because he is called simply "Father." That is membership in a body. The loss of the name in both cases reminds us that there are two opposite ways of departing from isolation.

The society into which the Christian is called at baptism is not a collective but a Body. It is in fact that Body of which the family is an image on the natural level. If anyone came to it with the misconception that membership of the Church was membership in a debased modern sense—a massing together of persons as if they were pennies or counters—he would be corrected at the threshold by the discovery that the head of this Body is so unlike the inferior members that they share no predicate with Him save by analogy. We are summoned from the outset to combine as creatures with our Creator, as mortals with immortal, as redeemed sinners with sinless Redeemer. His presence, the interaction between Him and us, must always be the overwhelmingly dominant factor in the life we are to lead within the Body, and any conception of Christian fellowship which does not mean primarily fellowship with Him is out of court. After that it seems almost trivial to trace further down the diversity of operations to the unity of the Spirit. But it is very plainly there. There are priests divided from the laity, catechumens divided from those who are in full fellowship. There is authority of husbands over wives and parents over children. There is, in forms too subtle for official embodiment, a continual interchange of complementary ministrations. We are all constantly teaching and learning, forgiving and being forgiven, representing Christ to man when we intercede, and man to Christ when others intercede for us. The sacrifice of selfish privacy which is daily demanded of us is daily repaid a hundredfold in the true growth of personality which the life of the Body encourages. Those who are members of one another become as diverse as the hand and the ear. That is why the worldlings are so monotonously alike compared with the almost fantastic variety of the saints. Obedience is the road to freedom, humility the road to pleasure, unity the road to personality.

And now I must say something that may appear to you a paradox. You have often heard that though in the world we hold different stations, yet we are all equal in the sight of God. There are, of course, senses in which this is true. God is no accepter of persons; His love for us is not measured by our social rank or our intellectual talents. But I believe there is a sense in which this maxim is the reverse of the truth. I am going to venture to say that artificial equality is necessary in the life of the State, but that in the Church we strip off this disguise, we recover our real inequalities, and are thereby refreshed and quickened.

I believe in political equality. But there are two opposite reasons for being a democrat. You may think all men so good that they deserve a share in the government of the commonwealth, and so wise that the commonwealth needs their advice. That is, in my opinion, the false, romantic doctrine of democracy. On the other hand, you may believe fallen men to be so wicked that not one of them can be trusted with any irresponsible power over his fellows.

That I believe to be the true ground of democracy. I do not believe that God created an egalitarian world. I believe the authority of parent over child, husband over wife, learned over simple to have been as much a part of the original plan as the authority of man over beast. I believe that if we had not fallen, Filmer would be right, and patriarchal monarchy would be the sole lawful government. But since we have learned sin, we have found, as Lord Acton says, that "all power corrupts, and absolute power corrupts absolutely." The only remedy has been to take away the powers and substitute a legal fiction of equality. The authority of father and husband has been rightly abolished on the legal plane, not because this authority is in itself bad (on the contrary, it is, I hold, divine in origin), but because fathers and husbands are bad. Theocracy has been rightly abolished not because it is bad that learned priests should govern ignorant laymen, but because priests are wicked men like the rest of us. Even the authority of man over beast has had to be interfered with because it is constantly abused.

Equality is for me in the same position as clothes. It is a result of the Fall and the remedy for it. Any attempt to retrace the steps by which we have arrived at egalitarianism and to reintroduce the old authorities on the political level is for me as foolish as it would be to take off our clothes. The Nazi and the nudist make the same mistake. But it is the naked body, still there beneath the clothes of each one of us, which really lives. It is the hierarchical world, still alive and (very properly) hidden behind a façade of equal citizenship, which is our real concern.

Do not misunderstand me. I am not in the least belittling the value of this egalitarian fiction which is our only defence against one another's cruelty. I should view with the strongest disapproval any proposal to abolish manhood suffrage, or the Married Women's Property Act. But the function of equality is purely protective. It is medicine, not food. By treating human persons (in judicious defiance of the observed facts) as if they were all the same kind of thing, we avoid innumerable evils. But it is not on this that we were made to live. It is idle to say that men are of equal value. If value is taken in a worldly sense—if we mean that all men are equally useful or beautiful or good or entertaining—then it is nonsense. If it means that all are of equal value as immortal souls, then I think it conceals a dangerous error. The infinite value of each human soul is not a Christian doctrine. God did not die for man because of some value He perceived in him. The value of each human soul considered simply in itself, out of relation to God, is zero. As St. Paul writes, to have died for valuable men would have been not divine but merely heroic; but God died for sinners. He loved us not because we were lovable, but because He is Love. It may be that He loves all equally—He certainly loved all to the death—and I am not certain what the expression means. If there is equality, it is in His love, not in us.

Equality is a quantitative term and therefore love often knows nothing of it. Authority exercised with humility and obedience accepted with delight are the very lines along which our spirits live. Even in the life of the affections, much more in the Body of Christ, we step outside that world which says "I am as good as you." It is like turning from a march to a dance. It is like taking off our clothes. We become, as Chesterton said, taller when we bow; we become lowlier when we instruct. It delights me that there should be moments in the services of my own Church when the priest stands and I kneel. As democracy becomes more complete in the outer world and opportunities for reverence are successively removed, the refreshment, the cleansing, and invigorating returns to inequality, which the Church offers us, become more and more necessary.

In this way then, the Christian life defends the single personality from the collective, not by isolating him but by giving him the status of an organ in the mystical Body. As the book of Revelation says, he is made "a pillar in the temple of God"; and it adds, "he shall go on more out." That introduces a new side of our subject. That structural position in the Church which the humblest Christian occupies is eternal and even cosmic. The Church will outlive the universe; in it the individual person will outlive the universe. Everything that is joined to the immortal head will share His immortality. We hear little of this from the Christian pulpit today. What has come of our silence may be judged from the fact that recently addressing the Forces on this subject, I found that one of my audience regarded this doctrine as "theosophical." If we do not believe it, let us be honest and relegate the Christian faith to museums. If we do, let us give up the pretence that it makes no difference. For this is the real answer to every excessive claim made by the collective. It is mortal; we shall live forever. There will come a time when every culture, every institution, every nation, the human race, all biological life is extinct and every one of us is still alive. Immortality is promised to us, not to these generalities. It was not for societies or states that Christ died, but for men. In that sense Christianity must seem to secular collectivists to involve an almost frantic assertion of individuality. But then it is not the individual as such who will share Christ's victory over death. We shall share the victory by being in the Victor. A rejection, or in Scripture's strong language, a crucifixion of the natural self is the passport to everlasting life. Nothing that has not died will be resurrected. That is just how Christianity cuts across the antithesis between individualism and collectivism. There lies the maddening ambiguity of our faith as it must appear to outsiders. It sets its face relentlessly against our natural individualism; on the other hand, it gives back to those who abandon individualism an eternal possession of their own personal being, even of their bodies. As mere biological entities, each with its separate will to live and to expand, we are apparently of no account; we are cross-fodder. But as organs in the Body of Christ, as stones and pillars in the temple, we are assured of our eternal self-identity and shall live to remember the galaxies as an old tale.

This may be put in another way. Personality is eternal and inviolable. But then, personality is not a datum from which we start. The individualism in which we all begin is only a parody or shadow of it. True personality lies ahead—how far ahead, for most of us, I dare not say. And the key to it does not lie in ourselves. It will not be attained by development from within outwards. It will come to us when we occupy those places in the structure of the eternal cosmos for which we were designed or invented. As a colour first reveals its true quality when placed by an excellent artist in its pre-elected spot between certain others, as a spice reveals its true flavour when inserted just where and when a good cook wishes among the other ingredients, as the dog becomes really doggy only when he has taken his place in the household of man, so we shall then first be true persons when we have suffered ourselves to be fitted into our places. We are marble waiting to be shaped, metal waiting to be run into a mould. No doubt there are already, even in the unregenerate self, faint hints of what mould each is designed for, or what sort of pillar he will be. But it is, I think, a gross exaggeration to picture the saving of a soul as being, normally, at all like the development from seed to flower. The very words *repentance, regeneration, the New Man*, suggest something very different. Some tendencies in each natural man may have to be simply rejected. Our Lord speaks of eyes being plucked out and hands lopped off—a frankly Procrustean method of adaptation.

The reason we recoil from this is that we have in our day started by getting the whole picture upside down. Starting with the doctrine that every individuality is "of infinite value," we then picture God as a kind of employment committee whose business it is to find suitable careers for souls, square holes for square pegs. In fact, however, the value of the individual does not lie in him. He is capable of receiving value. He receives it by union with Christ. There is no question of finding for him a place in the living temple which will do justice to his inherent value and give scope to his natural idiosyncrasy. The place was there first. The man was created for it. He will not be himself till he is there. We shall be true and everlasting and really divine persons only in Heaven, just as we are, even now, coloured bodies only in the light.

To say this is to repeat what everyone here admits already—that we are saved by grace, that in our flesh dwells no good thing, that we are, through and through, creatures not creators, derived beings, living not of ourselves but from Christ. If I seem to have complicated a simple matter, you will, I hope, forgive me. I have been anxious to bring out two points. I have wanted to try to expel that quite un-Christian worship of the human individual simply as such which is so rampant in modern thought side by side with our collectivism, for one error begets the opposite error and, far from neutralising, they aggravate each other. I mean the pestilent notion (one sees it in literary criticism) that each of us starts with a treasure called "personality" locked up inside him, and that to expand and express this, to guard it from interference, to be "original," is the main end of life. This is Pelagian, or worse, and it defeats even itself. No man who values originality will ever be original. But try to tell the truth as you see it, try to do any bit of work as well as it can be done for the work's sake, and what men call originality will come unsought. Even on that level, the submission of the individual to the function is already beginning to bring true personality to birth. And secondly, I have wanted to show that Christianity is not, in the long run, concerned either with individuals or communities. Neither the individual nor the community as popular thought understands them can inherit eternal life, neither the natural self, nor the collective mass, but a new creature.

ON FORGIVENESS

We say a great many things in church (and out of church too) without thinking of what we are saying. For instance, we say in the Creed "I believe in the forgiveness of sins." I had been saying it for several years before I asked myself why it was in the Creed. At first sight it seems hardly worth putting in. "If one is a Christian," I thought, "of course one believes in the forgiveness of sins. It goes without saying." But the people who compiled the Creed apparently thought that this was a part of our belief which we needed to be reminded of every time we went to church. And I have begun to see that, as far as I am concerned, they were right. To believe in the forgiveness of sins is not nearly so easy as I thought. Real belief in it is the sort of thing that very easily slips away if we don't keep on polishing it up.

We believe that God forgives us our sins; but also that He will not do so unless we forgive other people their sins against us. There is no doubt about the second part of this statement. It is in the Lord's Prayer; it was emphatically stated by our Lord. If you don't forgive you will not be forgiven. No part of His teaching is clearer, and there are no exceptions to it. He doesn't say that we are to forgive other people's sins provided they are not too frightful, or provided there are extenuating circumstances, or anything of that sort. We are to forgive them all, however spiteful, however mean, however often they are repeated. If we don't, we shall be forgiven none of our own.

Now it seems to me that we often make a mistake both about God's forgiveness of our sins and about the forgiveness we are told to offer to other people's sins. Take it first about God's forgiveness. I find that when I think I am asking God to forgive me I am often in reality (unless I watch myself very carefully) asking Him to do something quite different. I am asking Him not to forgive me but to excuse me. But there is all the difference in the world between forgiving and excusing. Forgiveness says "Yes, you have done this thing, but I accept your apology; I will never hold it against you and everything between us two will be exactly as it was before." But excusing says "I see that you couldn't help it or didn't mean it; you weren't really to blame." If one was not really to blame then there is nothing to forgive. In that sense forgiveness and excusing are almost opposites. Of course, in dozens of cases, either between God and man, or between one man and another, there may be a mixture of the two. Part of what seemed at first to be the sins turns out to be really nobody's fault and is excused; the bit that is left over is forgiven. If you had a perfect excuse, you would not need forgiveness; if the whole of your action needs forgiveness, then there was no excuse for it. But the trouble is that what we call "asking God's forgiveness" very often really consists in asking God to accept our excuses. What leads us into this mistake is the fact that there usually is some amount of excuse, some "extenuating circumstances." We are so very anxious to point these out to God (and to ourselves) that we are apt to forget the really important thing; that is, the bit left over, the bit which the excuses don't cover, the bit which is inexcusable but not, thank God, unforgivable. And if we forget this, we shall go away imagining that we have repented and been forgiven when all that has really happened is that we have satisfied ourselves with our own excuses. They may be very bad excuses; we are all too easily satisfied about ourselves.

There are two remedies for this danger. One is to remember that God knows all the real excuses very much better than we do. If there are real "extenuating circumstances" there is no fear that He will overlook them. Often He must know many excuses that we have never thought of, and therefore humble souls will, after death, have the delightful surprise of discovering that on certain occasions they sinned much less than they had thought. All the real excusing He will do. What we have got to take to Him is the inexcusable bit, the sin. We are only wasting time by talking about all the parts which can (we think) be excused. When you go to a doctor you show him the bit of you that is wrong —say, a broken arm. It would be a mere waste of time to keep on explaining that your legs and eyes and throat are all right. You may be mistaken in thinking so, and anyway, if they are really all right, the doctor will know that.

The second remedy is really and truly to believe in the forgiveness of sins. A great deal of our anxiety to make excuses comes from not really believing in it, from thinking that God will not take us to Himself again unless He is satisfied that some sort of case can be made out in our favour. But that would not be forgiveness at all. Real forgiveness means looking steadily at the sin, the sin that is left over without any excuse, after all allowances have been made, and seeing it in all its horror, dirt, meanness, and malice, and nevertheless being wholly reconciled to the man who has done it. That, and only that, is forgiveness, and that we can always have from God if we ask for it.

When it comes to a question of our forgiving other people, it is partly the same and partly different. It is the same because, here also, forgiving does not mean excusing. Many people seem to think it does. They think that if you ask them to forgive someone who has cheated or bullied them you are trying to make out that that there was really no cheating or no bullying. But if that were so, there would be nothing to forgive. They keep on replying, "But I tell you the man broke a most solemn promise." Exactly: that is precisely what you have to forgive. (This doesn't mean that you must necessarily believe his next promise. It does mean that you must make every effort to kill every taste of resentment in your own heart—every wish to humiliate or hurt him or to pay him out.) The difference between this situation and the one in which you are asking God's forgiveness is this. In our own case we accept excuses too easily; in other people's we do not accept them easily enough. As regards my own sins it is a safe bet (though not a certainty) that the excuses are not really so good as I think; as regards other men's since against me it is a safe bet (though not a certainty) that the excuses are better than I think. One must therefore begin by attending to everything which may show that the other man was not so much to blame as we thought. But even if he is absolutely fully to blame we still have to forgive him; and even if ninety-nine per cent of his apparent guilt can be explained away by really good excuses, the problem of forgiveness begins with the one per cent of guilt which is left over. To excuse what can really produce good excuses is not Christian charity; it is only fairness. To be a Christian means to forgive the inexcusable, because God has forgiven the inexcusable in you.

This is hard. It is perhaps not so hard to forgive a single great injury. But to forgive the incessant provocations of daily life—to keep on forgiving the bossy mother-in-law, the bullying husband, the nagging wife, the selfish daughter, the deceitful son— how can we do it? Only, I think, by remembering where we stand, by meaning our words when we say in our prayers each night "forgive us our trespasses as we forgive those that trespass against us." We are offered forgiveness on no other terms. To refuse it is to refuse God's mercy for ourselves. There is no hint of exceptions and God means what He says.

A SLIP
OF THE TONGUE

When a layman has to preach a sermon I think he is most likely to be useful, or even interesting, if he starts exactly from where he is himself, not so much presuming to instruct as comparing notes.

Not long ago when I was using the collect for the fourth Sunday after Trinity* in my private prayers I found that I had made a slip of the tongue. I had meant to pray that I might so pass through things temporal that I finally lost not the things eternal; I found I had prayed so to pass through things eternal that I finally lost not the things temporal. Of course, I don't think that a slip of the tongue is a sin. I am not sure that I am even a strict enough Freudian to believe that all such slips, without exception, are deeply significant. But I think some of them are significant, and I thought this was one of that sort. I thought that what I had inadvertently said very nearly expressed something I had really wished.

Very nearly; not, of course, precisely. I had never been quite stupid enough to think that the eternal could, strictly, be "passed through." What I had

---

* "O God, the protector of all that trust in thee, without whom nothing is strong, nothing is holy: Increase and multiply upon us thy mercy; that, through being our ruler and guide, we may so pass through things temporal, that we finally lose not the things eternal: Grant this, O heavenly Father, for Jesus Christ's sake our Lord. *Amen.*"—ed.

wanted to pass through without prejudice to my things temporal was those hours or moments in which I attended to the eternal, in which I exposed myself to it.

I mean this sort of thing. I say my prayers, I read a book of devotion, I prepare for, or receive, the Sacrament. But while I do these things, there is, so to speak, a voice inside me that urges caution. It tells me to be careful, to keep my head, not to go too far, not to burn my boats. I come into the presence of God with a great fear lest anything should happen to me within that presence which will prove too intolerably inconvenient when I have come out again into my "ordinary" life. I don't want to be carried away into any resolution which I shall afterwards regret. For I know I shall be feeling quite different after breakfast; I don't want anything to happen to me at the altar which will run up too big a bill to pay then. It would be very disagreeable, for instance, to take the duty of charity (while I am at the altar) so seriously that after breakfast I had to tear up the really stunning reply I had written to an impudent correspondent yesterday and meant to post today. It would be very tiresome to commit myself to a programme of temperance which would cut off my after-breakfast cigarette (or, at best, make it cruelly alternative to a cigarette later in the morning). Even repentance of past acts will have to be paid for. By repenting, one acknowledges them as sins—therefore not to be repeated. Better leave that issue undecided.

The root principle of all these precautions is the same: to guard the things temporal. And I find some evidence that this temptation is not peculiar to me. A good author (whose name I have forgotten) asks somewhere, "Have we never risen from our knees in haste for fear God's will should become too unmistakable if we prayed longer?" The following story was told as true. An Irish woman who had just been at confession met on the steps of the chapel the other woman who was her greatest enemy in the village. The other woman let fly a torrent of abuse. "Isn't it a shame for ye," replied Biddy, "to be talking to me like that, ye coward, and me in a state of Grace the way I can't answer ye? But you wait. I won't be in a state of Grace long." There is an excellent tragicomic example in Trollope's *Last Chronicle*. The Archdeacon was angry with his eldest son. He at once made a number of legal arrangements to the son's disadvantage. They could all easily have been made a few days later, but Trollope explains why the Archdeacon would not wait. To reach the next day, he had to pass through his evening prayers, and he knew that he might not be able to carry his hostile plans safely through the clause, "forgive us our trespasses as we forgive." So he got in first; he decided to present God with a *fait accompli*. This is an extreme case of the precautions I am talking about; the man will not venture within reach of the eternal until he has made the things temporal safe in advance.

This is my endlessly recurrent temptation: to go down to that Sea (I think St. John of the Cross called God a sea) and there neither dive nor swim nor float, but only dabble and splash, careful not to get out of my depth and holding on to the lifeline which connects me with my things temporal.

It is different from the temptations that met us **at** the beginning of the Christian life. Then we fought (at least I fought) against admitting the claims of the eternal at all. And when we had fought, and been beaten, and surrendered, we supposed that all would be fairly plain sailing. This temptation comes later. It is addressed to those who have already admitted the claim in principle and are even making some sort of effort to meet it. Our temptation is to look eagerly for the minimum that will be accepted. We are in fact very like honest but reluctant taxpayers. We approve of an income tax in principle. We make our returns truthfully. But we dread a rise in the tax. We are very careful to pay no more than is necessary. And we hope—we very ardently hope—that after we have paid it there will still be enough left to live on.

And notice that those cautions which the tempter whispers in our ears are all plausible. Indeed, I don't think he often tries to deceive us (after early youth) with a direct lie. The plausibility is this. It is really possible to be carried away by religious emotion—*enthusiasm* as our ancestors called it—into resolutions and attitudes which we shall, not sinfully but rationally, not when we are more worldly but when we are wiser, have cause to regret. We can become scrupulous or fanatical; we can, in what seems zeal but is really presumption, embrace tasks never intended for us. That is the truth in the temptation. The lie consists in the suggestion that our best protection is a prudent regard for the safety of our pocket, our habitual indulgences, and our ambitions. But that is quite false. Our real protection is to be sought elsewhere: in common Christian usage, in moral theology, in steady rational thinking, in the advice of good friends and good

books, and (if need be) in a skilled spiritual director.
Swimming lessons are better than a lifeline to the
shore.

For of course that lifeline is really a death line.
There is no parallel to paying taxes and living on
the remainder. For it is not so much of our time
and so much of our attention that God demands; it
is not even all our time and all our attention; it is
ourselves. For each of us the Baptist's words are
true: "He must increase and I decrease." He will
be infinitely merciful to our repeated failures; I
know no promise that He will accept a deliberate
compromise. For He has, in the last resort, nothing
to give us but Himself; and He can give that only
insofar as our self-affirming will retires and makes
room for Him in our souls. Let us make up our
minds to it; there will be nothing "of our own"
left over to live on, no "ordinary" life. I do not
mean that each of us will necessarily be called to be
a martyr or even an ascetic. That's as may be. For
some (nobody knows which) the Christian life will
include much leisure, many occupations we naturally like. But these will be received from God's
hands. In a perfect Christian they would be as
much part of his "religion," his "service," as his
hardest duties, and his feasts would be as Christian
as his fasts. What cannot be admitted—what must
exist only as an undefeated but daily resisted enemy—is the idea of something that is "our own,"
some area in which we are to be "out of school,"
on which God has no claim.

For He claims all, because He is love and must
bless. He cannot bless us unless He has us. When
we try to keep within us an area that is our own,

we try to keep an area of death. Therefore, in love, He claims all. There's no bargaining with Him.

That is, I take it, the meaning of all those sayings that alarm me most. Thomas More said, "If ye make indentures with God how much ye will serve Him, ye shall find ye have signed both of them yourself." Law, in his terrible, cool voice, said, "Many will be rejected at the last day, not because they have taken no time or pains about their salvation, but because they have not taken time and pains enough"; and later, in his richer, Behmenite period, "If you have not chosen the Kingdom of God, it will make in the end no difference what you have chosen instead." Those are hard words to take. Will it really make no difference whether it was women or patriotism, cocaine or art, whisky or a seat in the Cabinet, money or science? Well, surely no difference that matters. We shall have missed the end for which we are formed and rejected the only thing that satisfies. Does it matter to a man dying in a desert by which choice of route he missed the only well?

It is a remarkable fact that on this subject Heaven and Hell speak with one voice. The tempter tells me, "Take care. Think how much this good resolve, the acceptance of this Grace, is going to cost." But Our Lord equally tells us to count the cost. Even in human affairs great importance is attached to the agreement of those whose testimony hardly ever agrees. Here, more. Between them it would seem to be pretty clear that paddling is of little consequence. What matters, what Heaven desires and Hell fears, is precisely that further step, out of our depth, out of our own control.

And yet, I am not in despair. At this point I become what some would call very Evangelical; at any rate very un-Pelagian. I do not think any efforts of my own will can end once and for all this craving for limited liabilities, this fatal reservation. Only God can. I have good faith and hope He will. Of course, I don't mean that I can therefore, as they say, "sit back." What God does for us, He does in us. The process of doing it will appear to me (and not falsely) to be the daily or hourly repeated exercises of my own will in renouncing this attitude, especially each morning, for it grows all over me like a new shell each night. Failures will be forgiven; it is acquiescence that is fatal, the permitted, regularised presence of an area in ourselves which we still claim for our own. We may never, this side of death, drive the invader out of our territory, but we must be in the Resistance, not in the Vichy government. And this, so far as I can yet see, must be begun again every day. Our morning prayer should be that in the *Imitation: Da hodie perfecte incipere* —grant me to make an unflawed beginning today, for I have done nothing yet.